How survive travelling in Australia

first-hand advice, anecdotes + warnings
for young travellers and armchair explorers

Rainer Krauhs

Copyright © 2015 Rainer Krauhs

All rights reserved.

ISBN: 1497462797
ISBN-13: 978-1497462793

Die deutsche Fassung ist erschienen als:
A German version is available as:
ISBN: 1519349904
ISBN-13: 978-1519349903

Legal notice:
Neither author nor any party that partook in getting this book to you are liable for any damage, fatalities, expenses or fun missed arising, or not arising, from following, or not following, the security tips provided in this book. These are purely meant to alert the reader to the heightened possibility of danger, and inspire the reader to reflect upon and potentially take special security measures. Any action or non-action, and consequences thereof, is at the full discretion and liability of the reader.

CONTENTS

      Introduction   1

1. Stationary hazards   3
2. Dangers When Getting Around   96
3. The Good Stories   145

(Australian winter that is). Now, while you're out shopping, slap on some extra and invest in body lotion to feed your sun-dried stressed-out skin at the end of the day. You'll thank yourself if your aging skin starts to shrivel late.

In winter there's snow in the Australian Alps. Skiing is only good in the mornings –due to the strong sun. By noon it's slushy like a Daiquiri. The reason being: During winter, the UV index in Australia is at 9 and above – three times that of Europe during summer. Better equip yourself with a hat and clothes that cover you all over. And wear them. If you didn't bring them, never mind – there are department stores. For dress code, consider Australian school uniforms as role model. Many Australian schools are state-sponsored "sun-smart schools" where outdoor grounds are shaded by awnings, windows are tinted and despite the heat school uniforms include long clothes and hats with veils covering wearers' necks.

Let's talk about beach life. Seeing people wear hats and long bathing attire or neoprene suits out of the water – despite high temperatures – and white zinc paste (protection factor somewhere above 70 or so) on their noses might be an uncommon sight to visitors, but not in Australia where you've got to defend your skin. Long clothes are non-expiring protections from the sun that don't wash off. Noses stick out from under hats. Yet all this taking protective measures isn't without measurable consequences as scientists found out: Statistics show that the average Australian parent lets their kids wear neoprene suits to the beach (these are available from wherever kids' clothes are sold). This is so common that scientists were able to collect a sufficiently large body of data to empirically prove that the heat trapped under this kind of suit decreases kids' growth. A startling fact – but do parents really have a choice, considering the health threat from UV radiation?

You have a choice. Choose to learn from others' failures! Such as those of cliché British tourists. Australians enjoy both coining new terms for what they see and picking on the British (certainly due to the shared history that connects these two countries). Consequently, there's an expression in Australian English for all-male groups of young British travellers: "red diamonds" – because that's what can frequently be seen on the backs of young British men travelling with male mates who've failed to apply sunscreen onto their own back themselves and have opted to refrain from asking their mates for the favor for worry that any onlookers might be misinterpreting the gesture.

Water

Have plenty of drinking water with you, and drink lots of it very frequently. The moment you think you've packed enough water you've solely packed the absolute minimum, so take this as a hint to stock up with even more water. As a traveller you're lucky that Australians understand you need water as much as air to breath – anyone I approached asking for water gave it to me for free! Most of them were being so kind to even take care themselves of cleaning, drying, filling up and wiping dry off my water bottle as a matter of course. I always deemed that very generous and thanked them – but they always shrugged that off; to them, sharing water with those needing it is just commonplace as it can be a matter of life or death.

To the four Frenchmen that left Perth together with me it was the first time that they departed from Just Another Big City and into the Outback – in other words: into the real Australia. Each of them only carried a tiny

INTRODUCTION

"For those about to rock – we salute you"
(AC/DC, Australian rock band)

Dear reader,
It's been eleven years since I returned from Australia.

I'm lucky because I returned safe and healthy. Back then, I was a naive young man. Very naive. Only in retrospect did I realize just how lucky I was: Many times, I dodged dangerous situations by pure coincidence. Other times, I intuitively applied common sense.

I am thankful to all deities and guardian angels, and to the people whom I've met in my travels for making it a safe event.

So here I am – finally sharing what I learned, to support you on your way – so that you may seize the opportunity and grow as a person through travelling. Read from this book and choose from my advice as you like. Just remember to make it through your travels healthy and alive.
To support my advice, and for the entertainment of those staying home or seeking to whet their appetite for travel, I'm providing first-hand anecdotes through which I learned those recommendations.

For readers impatient or just browsing, I here summarize the advice I deem most important:
- Take preventive measures in advance.
- What is unsafe to do at home is unsafe away from home.
- Let someone you trust know where you're going so they can alert someone should you not arrive as

planned. Tell them who to call – and then sign out with them as soon as you're back in safety.
- Read warning signs and follow their advice. Someone has spent money and effort to put them there to save you. Recognize places and situations where no warning sign has been put up but should have been.
- Drink plenty of water. Bring sufficient supplies.
- Wear sunscreen.

1. STATIONARY HAZARDS

My subjective, incomplete list of hazards that you may encounter while travelling in Australia begins with: you. Because, as always in grown-up life, you're the person who is most responsible for keeping yourself safe. Only then does the list continue with other people, and the organizations people form. The reason for that being: Can you trust others as much as you can trust yourself? Like, seriously? The list goes on with animals and nature – there are lots of both in Australia and they are likely to be very different from what you're accustomed to from the place you come from. Both can be much more dangerous than animals and nature are elsewhere (especially that civilized town you're accustomed to live in). Finally, the list concludes with hazards while getting around – you're not intending to travel to Australia and then stay put in one spot, are you? Just in case you do: Some hazards themselves do travel, and they might be heading towards where ever you are.

Hazards – yourself

This section lists the mere basics you can follow to keep yourself alive and healthy under circumstances that are specific to Australia.

Sunscreen
Wear sunscreen. Lots of sunscreen. Imagine showering in it – daily. Consider protection factor 50+ the bare

minimum and chose one far above that – sporting a white smear for a few minutes is so much better than getting a sunburn or post-operation scars for a lifetime from treatment of skin cancer or prematurely aged skin or a terminal illness. Put a bottle of sunscreen on your bedside table (or wherever you can reach it fast after waking up) and make it a habit to put it on the moment you wake – about 30 minutes before you go outdoors for the first time (it requires that time to bond with the skin; lip sunscreen needs up to 60 minutes). Ensure you always have a second bottle as spare in case you lose the first one or it runs dry unexpectedly (to dodge the risk of getting sunburned while shopping for a replacement). Reapply every two hours. Wear long clothes, a hat and sunglasses that meet Australian Standards. Seek shade and apply extra care around noon. (These recommendations courtesy of Cancer Council Australia – does that name ring a bell? – with my own additions.)

Having arrived to Australia in Sydney, I spent one of my first days visiting museums. Most of that day I sojourned indoors or on underground subway trains. It was a cloudy, foggy day somewhen in winter, but by the end of it I found I had a tan. Australia lies under the famous hole in our atmosphere's ozone layer. Any questions?

As weird as it may sound – there's an upside thanks to this: Sunscreen with sufficient protection is expensive in many places, but not in Australia. Thus, when voyaging to Australia you only need to take enough with you to protect yourself until you can make it to a supermarket to stock up on supplies. Sunscreen is available year-round in all supermarkets and a couple of other places – in packs up to 5 liters (sounds impressive, right? But then those are just the family value packs), and only in the midst of winter will sunscreen be on sale

Make a conscious effort to make it back home alive and healthy!

water bottle that contained nothing more than a few quick gulps. When I advised they needed more than that for a day on the road they disagreed, stating that they believed they'd be all right telling from their life experience (collected however solely outsides of Australia) that this would suffice them for a whole day. Yet we weren't going places they've been before but making our way straight into the Outback! What followed was an entire day of travel. Upon meeting up again on the next morning, they had discarded their tiny bottles for more apt ones. They now all sported identically shaped 2.5-liter lemonade bottles. Every single one of those had all labels scraped off meticulously. To be able to tell the bottles apart nonetheless, they had color coded the water: Each had mixed in a different flavor of flashy, artificially colored cordial: red, yellow, green and blue, agleam like Christmas decoration.

Can 2 liters per day do? Once I drove by car from Longreach towards Three Ways. The car's air conditioning was broken, so my fellow travellers and me drove with the windows down. It was hot, but we weren't sweating at all – and neither were we shivering, due to the constant wind blast coming in being comfortably warm. I drank about 9 liters that day. In the evening, we stopped in the parking lot of a roadhouse, got out and ambled around taking in the surroundings, I noted my co-travellers t-shirts were soaked with sweat – but only at the back where they had been leaning against their seats. I couldn't help but take a closer look. Those areas were each surrounded by a broad, limy strip of dried-in sweat. It took me a moment to discover: The back of the t-shirt I wore looked just the same. It had been so hot I had been sweating without noticing it, because all of it had evaporated immediately. That very moment, a convoy of trucks that hauled parts of a yet-to-be-assembled windmill power plant pulled into the parking lot and halted in the bays next to us. Trucks and plant were all painted in a uniform snow white with not a single marking. We had seen them on the road that day several times, us overtaking them or vice versa. Each time, their spacious cabins caught my eye – walled with tinted windows and unusually large and edgy almost as big as like shipping containers. These cabins must have been equipped with perfectly working air conditioning (as required by Australian work safety laws that define a maximum workplace temperature) – quite obviously, because the next moment the cabin doors were opened, the drivers and passengers lent forward into the air and climbed down the ladders like angels descending from heaven. Upon them touching ground and strolling around taking in the surroundings among us mere mortals, I noted ashamed that the way they looked differed so much from us as if they had only just gotten up, showered and put on freshly laundered and pressed clothes.

Can 9 liters per day do? On the way from Yulara to Alice Springs, I was travelling with tourists on a guided bus tour. At each stop or break we got free water – every other hour there were breaks even in case there was nothing near or far to be looked at. The bus simply pulled over for everyone to stretch their legs, and always a small group would hang about and mingle by the front door, waiting for the driver or tour guide to give us the get-go for jumping back on the bus so we could continue to keep heading onwards for the horizon and beyond. During those breaks, our always very kind driver would cordially hand out small plastic cups to everyone within close reach, filling those from a water tank that resided behind an opening cover on the buses' side. Eventually, during one of those breaks – everyone else was in full activity with casually sipping the free water, looking at nothing specific in the surroundings and idling around lost in their thought, that water tank caught my eye. For the first time I noted that it looked larger that I had believed, seemingly extending far beyond the opening cover. I switched my position, moved closer and bent down to get a proper look, and only then were able to properly see exactly how far – and deep – it extended into the belly of the bus. I realized: under our seats this bus was moving around a whole cistern of our very own! That gargantuan tank contained about two cubic meters! It wasn't there for casually dishing out small cups of water to idle travellers every now and then. It was there to save our lives in case the bus broke down and the scorching sun and lack of nearby infrastructure and technical help (typical to Australia) put us into mortal danger. In Australia, it gets hot and it's too far to walk as settlements and roadhouses – if they're there at all – are 100 kilometers to 200 kilometers or more apart.

Stay with the car
Imagine you find yourself travelling in the outback by car. Something happens so that you cannot continue driving and you need help – what do you do? Plain vanilla: Stay put with the car and wait until help comes along. Because a car is very resourceful in the outback: It provides shade from the sun. It stores all supplies you brought that you cannot carry around; especially your water reserves – always bring much more water than you can carry as you'll need all of it, did I mention that? A car shields you from sandstorms, animals and nighttime freezing temperatures. Even if it doesn't move an inch, in the outback a properly equipped car is your lifeline back into civilization's welcoming embrace.
Plus: A car is better visible from airplanes. Seen from above, a person is just a black dot in an area full of black dots, but a car is a shiny colorful rectangle that throws a

long shadow onto a shadowless plain. Thus, rescue searchers are able to spot a car much quicker than they can spot a person – especially if that person lies still due to dehydration.

"The Lucky One" was a newspaper headline which one day all major newspapers bore: on their front page, superimposed over a large photo. It had been taken from a helicopter and thus was a difficult to decipher at first look: zoomed in on a man's face, yet capturing it only partially; next to it was a white rectangle like a space intentionally left blank. Only after reading the accompanying article were I able to see on it: a man standing next to a 4WD that was bogged down in a sand dune. While looking straight up at the helicopter that hovered above him, he shaded his eyes from the sun. Even then I was still puzzled at the headline – until I found out I had completely missed the unfolding drama that climaxed in that photo moment since I hadn't at all followed the news during the days before. The whole story, as I then learned included not just the lucky one but actually two people and it had went like this: At the same time, two different men, both travelling by themselves in 4WD cars, had gone missing, one in the Western Australia desert, the other one in the dunes region north of Darwin. Both men had been tourists from out of country. Neither knew how to properly drive a 4WD vehicle off-road (similar to too many tourists when they set off to tour Australia). Rescue teams had been searching for both men. The Lucky One was found soon because he had stayed with his car. The other one had tried to walk 55 kilometers in the heat back towards a roadhouse he had passed by earlier. By dusk rescue workers in an airplane had discovered his car (which contained his stock of about 120 liters of drinking water – enough to fill a bathtub), but soon thereafter dusk fell and the search had to be paused due to an oncoming sandstorm. Early the next morning the man himself was found. Descendants of native Australians – who had volunteered to help in the search and were familiar with both the area and outdoor survival – had been sifting through the areas left and right of the road. He was still 25 kilometers away from the roadhouse. He was carrying with him only two (now entirely empty) water bottles, maugre he had managed to walk 30 kilometers under the scorching sun – and in doing so he had gotten so dehydrated he was unconscious when found, unable to take a nip from the provisions the volunteers providently had packed and schlepped for him and perished soon.

Travel together in pairs or groups
If you're together with someone else, you build memories to share and can split the costs. You've always got caring friends nearby, thus saving the effort to frequently make new ones (or fend off wannabees). And there's always someone who can go for help if needed.

Did you see that movie 127 hours – or read the book? It's the true story of a man travelling by himself – and it's similar to what a hiker endured in Australia (who, however, didn't publish a book that went on to become a Hollywood movie). He went bushwalking alone (that is: hiking through wilderness in a location remote from any civilization, settlements or other persons – this includes marked and maintained hiking paths in national parks) and ended up with an arm jammed between fallen rocks. Even though he was close to a marked hiking trail in a popular national park, no one found him because even by comparison oft-visited places with civilized infrastructure are lonely places. There simply was no one else around to hear his calls for help. Park rangers do patrol hiking paths, however they stick to hiking paths (which they maintain when they're not busy tending to visitors) and he had ventured off of it, instead of following the rangers' guideline to "Stay on the path" (because that's where they look for people potentially in distress since they assume you'd follow their guideline). Eventually, after 72 hours of waiting in despair, he decided to undertake drastic measures to free himself and ensure his (albeit partial) survival.

Tell someone where you're going and whom to notify if you don't check in, and contact them as soon as you've returned to safety – so they may send help your way in case you don't

Always telling someone your plans ensures that if you do go missing help will be dispatched quickly and that rescuers will know where you're most likely to be found and should thus be searching for you first. For some extremely remote areas in the desert that is even required by law, so should you want to venture out into those areas prepare yourself by informing yourself about whom to inform – and then do inform them. Usually your point of contact for those travelling into those areas is the police, who rents out two-way radio for constantly keeping in touch with them. For any other area, may it be remote or not, choosing and instructing your persons of contact is entirely your task. By the way, did I already mention that in Australia any area outside of a large city is remote?

Every year hundreds of people disappear in Australia permanently. Notice boards in hotels and hostels frequently have search notes for people missing, complete with pictures and information what clothes they had been wearing and where they had been seen last. None of them left notices or at least hints where they wanted to go or where to look for them, so make sure you do or – in if the worst comes to the worst – you'll be missed dearly.

Protect yourself from insect bites

There are mosquitoes in Australia (called "mozzies" by the locals – Australians have a thing for modifying words so much until they start to sound cute). These are far more aggressive than the ones you might know from other places. So, wear clothing that covers you well (this is also a good protection against sunburn – did I already mention that?). Use insect repellent and make sure it's a chemical one since flowery natural ones only make you smell nice but are no match for Australian mozzies. Consequently, chemical insect repellent is much cheaper in Australia than wherever you fly in from.

I had bread with Marmite for breakfast each day, because scientists had proven that this reduces insect bites by about 80%. (I did that in addition to applying sunscreen and DEET-containing insect repellent daily immediately after rising.) That lead to Australians which witnessed me doing that making astonished comments of how I was the first-ever German they saw who ate Marmite voluntarily. Quite understandable: If you're not accustomed to Marmite ... well, despite the looks it's not Nutella (a very sweet bread spread much favored in Germany – it's many people's childhood staple, just like Marmite is to many Australians), so spread Marmite as thinly as you can to thin down its taste if you're not used to it. As I happened to observe in myself and others, it's possible to assert – with absolute certainty – if someone is from Germany and having breakfast in Australia for the first time solely by: a) the massive layer of Marmite which they spread onto their bread (since in that moment they believe that in this faraway country they found a

Nutella look-alike very much reminding of home – looking forward to the treat and to a small cure for homesickness), b) their facial expression freezing in shock and disbelief the moment they bite into it and their tastebuds tell them it's not sweet as expected but antipodal to that and c) their subsequent behavior of not going near that once bitten-off slice of bread again!

Read warning signs. Read commemorative signs.

All around the country, you'll find plenty of warning signs – but not in all places where dangerous situations exist. This is important to know, especially for the out-of-countryers who happen to not yet have realized the dangers that are all around them. So read the signs carefully, consider what they want to convey to you, and make an effort to recognize places and situations where no warning sign exists but should. That way, you'll be doing a favor to all of yourself, the people who've put money and effort into the signs through which they try to keep you safe and the people who'd come to your help if needed even if that would mean they would be putting themselves at risk.

Australians are great at putting up commemorative displays. Consider this (at first seemingly amusing) example: There's a simple three-way road intersection somewhere in the Northern Territory. Next to it stands a waist-high monolith commemorating it's opening ceremony, naming (with all his titles) the minister who cut the rope and officially declared it open. Quite a bit overhyped for an intersection? What is it named anyways? "Three-Ways". Just that. Inventive – not at all. All the same this intersection appears – along with its simple name – on pretty much every map of the continent. Essentially, that simple name isn't even necessary to clearly distinguish it, since it's the one and only major road intersection for hundreds of kilometers. That's how remote and far-off you can get in Australia.

As mentioned, Australians are great at putting up signs that convey warnings or commemorations of the deceased. Here are select highlights of their inscriptions that I came across in person:

"He came for a break – and stayed forever," says a commemorative marble plaque for a young man put up by his family. While on a journey, they took a break on a small rest area at the rim of a Queensland national park. The young man climbed around the large, round grinded boulders that filled an adjacent, almost dry river bed. But suddenly he fell and became stuck – just when when a flash flood struck, filling up the river bed.

"Seven people have died here – don't be the eighth one," warns the last line of an explanatory sign at the shore of a lake south of Launceston. That sign declares that while the lake might appear tranquil and harmless, it really is a side exit of a dam several kilometers away. Under the lake's surface, turbine pipes discharge into it. These may be activated as needed at any time without advance warning, causing heavy currents. The volume of water that such pipes move can't be estimated to low: While the dam exit into that lake lies under water (with no pipes to be seen anywhere near of far), at another one further south I got to see pipes out in the open. There seemed to be as many as there are twigs in a tangled shrubbery – each of them five meters in diameter – and they all dropped straight down several hundred meters from a mountain. Imagine the masses of water those pipes could carry (and the speed the steep decline would give them), and the currents it would cause.

"Steven, we love you!" – "Steven, you're our best friend!" – "Steven, we miss you!" – these messages are spray-painted in green (together with the senders' signatures) onto huge boulders that sit alongsides a road upon which most drivers go way too fast. It's a steep and narrow road that winds down from the Atherton Tablelands. It has no shoulder, no stopping bays, no lighting – and no fencing from the cliff right next to it. And because it's a busy main road, slowing down at one's own discretion is difficult without becoming a hazard to those following closely behind you.

"Do not start this walk if the thermometer shows more than 30°C on or after 10am" advise signs at the trail outsets for Uluru and for Kings Canyon. Both are located right in the middle of a desert. Those signs actually are equipped with thermometers – and their messages are repeated in ten different languages (with the translations being of very high quality as far as I can tell), to warn all the tourists flying in from all over the world to the nearby airport – that is, from their safe home regions with climates of moderate temperatures straight into the extreme heat of the desert in only a few hours. As long as the sun is in the sky, temperatures on the ground keep rising. So, if it's 30°C hot early in the day, at noon and thereafter the heat will dehydrate you before you can return and get yourself back into safety. No, there are neither infrastructure nor shortcuts left or right to any hiking paths. These only lead you straight into the heart of the wilderness.

...and after you've read aforementioned sign that stands next to Uluru, you'd certainly like to count and consider the number of marble displays fastened to it at the trail outset – that is, before starting to ponder whether or not it's a good idea to climb the roof of the Aborigines' cathedral and to possibly follow those who did so before you and never returned back down to earth.

The aforementioned examples cite signs which contain hints, thus requiring you to think and imagine to understand their warnings. Yet only a minor part of warning signs was written in such a way that you would need to think about their intentions before grasping their meaning. The majority is quite forthright, such as warning signs from crocodiles in Kakadu National Park. These bear easy to decipher icons and are meticulously placed next to waterbodies and rivers where crocodiles live. However, despite the vast number of warning signs in Australia, only a minor part of dangers has warnings signs of their own. As concerns Kakadu NP and crocodiles, a lot of the park consists of shallow wetlands or other flat areas which get submerged during the wet season. Crocodiles grab that opportunity by its horns and settle into those areas, be that by swimming or by walking (crocodiles are able to traverse over dry ground), thus making them no-go zones – potential death traps. In Australia there are far more crocodile-infested areas than crocodile warning signs, and they even exist close to human settlements such as the beaches of Port Douglas or billabongs within the City of Cairns.

Finally, not all warning signs are about lethal dangers Some just spread useful advice. So do signs along the road to Wyndham's Five River Lookout. They warn against the long, steep incline that's too much for most cars. Nonetheless I attempted driving up there in our car, but the road up the hill goes mostly straight. The engine temperature gauge went up into the red quicker than rushing clocks in time travel movies, so we gave up driving, parked the car on the side of the road and walked the remainder (which was actually farther than we had gotten with the car). Up there from the lookout (that features a large car park and a meteorological station), we got to enjoy the panoramic views over the unifying river deltas. A couple pulled in by car up there. We struck up a conversation with them amazed about them making it, considering our own car troubles. They kindly offered us a ride back down to save us the return walk – they hadn't had any trouble with their car when they drove up the incline. It was a Ute (a utility vehicle type that occurs only in Australia – front part: passenger car, back part: flatbed truck), and we got to sit in the only space left: on the back at the open air, next to their dogs and squashed between their furniture (the two were just moving houses). From there, we could look both at the scenery some more as well as at the trailer that this Ute was pulling on top of it all (it was stuffed with two motorcycles and plenty of moving boxes). Different from our car, their Ute could had transported all that and still made it up. On our way down in the back of that Ute, the moments flew by and after an almost unnoticeable short amount of time we were down already. Next to our parked ordinary car we jumped off, said our goodbyes to the couple and then drove the short remainder of the road ourselves. Compared to the stretch of road which we had covered in the Ute (which different from our car it had managed to drive up), that bit on which our car's engine temperature had skyrocketed into the red now looked unimpressively brief and flat.

This ends the section on risks that you can easily dodge by carefully considering and choosing your whereabouts and actions. Next is: risks coming at you from where you might not expect.

Hazards – people

Life is basically the same everywhere on earth (I first heard that observation from an Iowan with whom I happened to discuss love relationships). However, people and cultures in different regions bear different attitudes and experiences. I were once explained how cultural shocks came about to be – according to that, they occur because everywhere on earth people's lives are about 95% similar, so when you eventually come across something from the remaining 5%, the dissimilarity is totally unexpected, hits you as a shock because you've grown so accustomed to the similarities in life.

Now these 5% potentially can be especially detrimental to you, because while you already might be mentally prepared for poisonous animals and adverse climate (cliché Australian dangers) here's some information on risks coming from an avenue you might not expect: other people.

Not being concerned with whom an item belongs to

Colonization of Australia began with the deportation of jailed British criminals into areas taken away from the people that lived there before – British government officials intended to thin out the number of poor people. Thus, the sentence of deportation was given even for petty crimes. People stayed and flourished – both liberated criminals and former guards. This beginning of modern Australian society has occurred several generations ago. Nowadays convict colonies only exist as ruins in open air museums, plus in the drawn-out meantime many more people from all over the world immigrated to Australia. What kind of society is it today? Which views and values do these people hold? Are they always people-friendly?

Late one night, I got dropped off on the side of the interstate road that runs past Coober Pedy. Standing there for a moment before setting off to head into town, I noted that by chance the outer shell of a mobile phone was lying close to where I was standing. I wondered if there was more to be found and started to look around. About a meter further I stumbled upon phone's interior. I assembled the pieces and switched it on – it was still working well. I wondered if there was a way to find out about its owner who quite might be missing it – I rummaged around its menu, found an address book, browsed the stored phone numbers and immediately stopped when coming across an entry labeled "Mom, mobile". I pushed the dial button and held the phone to my ear, my gaze falling onto the deserted road leading past sleeping Coober Pedy which was about two kilometers away and spread out across some wavy narrow hills. An unsuspecting woman took answered and I explained her the reasons for my call. With much concern in her voice she identified herself as the mother of the owner who was en route to Darwin. She asked me to mail the phone to her at her own expense, so she could return it to her daughter. I duly wrote down her address (she was on Tasmania) for which she seemed to be relieved and thankful. Early the very next morning, I brought the phone to the local postal office and sent it off in packing material which was on sale there. Figuring that someone living on Tasmania might rarely receive mail from Coober Pedy, I even added a picture postcard at my own expense, writing her kind greetings. Then I went shopping at the supermarket right next to the postal office. Mere moments later, by chance I met a new acquaintance at the checkout whom I first had met the evening before. I narrated to her my experience with the lost property as it was fresh on my mind, intending to share the joy of returning a lost object to its owner. But before I was halfway finished with the story – before I could get to the point where I mailed the phone back – she interrupted me as if believing I were done, asking me with a serious face "How much did you get?" as if expecting me to have done nothing else but sell it.

Now confusingly, at the postal office, when I asked whether I should mail the phone insured the postal agent told me that doing so wasn't necessary since Australia Post doesn't lose a single thing, whereas when I later mailed a parcel from Europe to Australia insured, I had to seal it with wax by requirement set forth by – Australia Post! It looked to me like according to their experience they felt they could trust only their own crew.

If anybody finds a black G-Star brand backpack within the Darwin region, containing (among other things) a notebook, please return it to me. I forgot it on the terrace seating area of a food outlet. When I later returned to fetch it, it was gone. The people which ran the place had seen it – and seen as well about eight to nine people who've walked past the table under which my backpack was lying in plain view. But they didn't bother picking it up to keep it safe for me. Someone else took it – and kept it. That really hurt my feelings, even more so since the notebook was the sole exchange of contact data between close friends I had made in Australia and me.

Rip-off

If you buy a service, make sure it's done properly!
Car repairs: Check if the garage is of good reputation and have them show you proof that their service was carried out at all. Consider turning to an Automobile Association to get help with both.
Car buying: Have a specialist check and confirm whether it is in good working order and ready to last you a couple thousand kilometers.
Offers: check if any claims made are reasonable and correct. Only then is it likely that whatever you purchase will live up to the promises and be of good quality.

One night in Thredbo I awoke from loud howling and screeching noises that came from a car outsides; from the car park next to where I lodged. The noise was ongoing and I lay in bed for endless minutes stretching into the pitch black eternity of night, waiting for the noise to go go away so I could go back to sleep (two pillows stacked onto my ears didn't provide enough cushion from the rumble). Since it didn't – the car didn't drove away and neither was it turned off – I eventually left my comfy warm bed, threw on clothing (quickly, since the room was unheated and the ground was as cold as ice so that I balanced on one leg until I had put on my winter boots) and went outside looking for the source of the caterwauling. In the car park between hotel and employee barracks, a group of people had gathered, standing between the source of the noise and me. I walked towards them and, as I got closer, could see what was in their midst: an old blue VW bug. The driver was in his seat trying everything possible to get the car to move, however it stubbornly remained stationary as if frozen into place. Despite the large volume of engine noise it emitted, it didn't budge a single inch. All the while the driver had his door wide open, talking to bystanders. I neared to him and asked for an explanation of the noise in specific and the odd scene in general. He, seemingly puzzled and perplexed, described with many gestures that he was trying to put the car into gear and go, yet he hadn't succeeded in anything he had tried towards that end (up until that moment, this task seemed rather simple to me). While talking, he had gotten out and freed the drivers' seat for his partner; she didn't succeed likewise. Finally, at the end of his explanation, he offered to let me try! He actually wanted a total stranger, whom he only just had met, take the wheel of his car! Altruistic as I am and longing to go back to sleep as I were, I accepted that challenge on the spot and with pleasure. He complimented his partner out; she stepped asides and I bowed down and slid into the confined space between steering wheel and driver's seat. It was my first time insides a VW bug – one sits quite low and, thanks to the spring padding, very comfy. To put the car in motion, I pushed the pedals and then moved the gear shift as usual. But there – that moment, in that car – it felt like I was moving a long spoon around through a large bowl of pudding and, different from what I had learned to expect from gearboxes, there was no gear or any other differentiation of whatever kind to be found. Astonished, I felt the urge to mention that observation to the owner-driver, so I turned my head towards where I had seen him last – looked over my shoulder and out the door that still stood ajar – however by that moment the owner of the hotel nearby had arrived on the scene. He asked for clarification of the noise disturbing the sleep of his and surrounding hotel's guests. He was offered the same explanation as me as well as a go at putting the VW bug into gear – his go lead to identical result as mine. Upon getting out, he promptly congratulated the owner-driver couple for their luck of having car trouble right in front of the only hotel in an overbooked ski resort town that had a room available. So finally the car was powered off – silence, at last! We (the driver, the hotel owner, the other onlookers and me) pushed it into a free parking slot and everyone headed into different directions. The next morning, the VW bug got towed to the local garage. Two days later I re-encountered its owners at the hotel's breakfast buffet. They were skiing teachers from Italy and had flown in for the winter season to give lessons in Thredbo. That VW bug was new to them; they had purchased it at a used car dealership straight after arriving to Australia via Sydney Airport, then taken it on the 500 kilometers long drive to Cooma and up into the mountains past Jindabyne. Its gearbox, as the local garage found out, had been glued together with silicone. The two Italians were lucky their new used car had broken down only after they had reached their destination – even more so since Australian alpine roads too are deserted, especially in winter when snowstorms overwhelm them on a regular basis.

I would dare to say that their good fortune was even larger since they didn't took their wreck of a car into the hot, dry desert. Because that's what two friends of a mutual friend of mine had done with their station wagon, getting them into plenty of trouble. They set off for the outback after having had their car serviced in a Cairns garage. There they were billed plenty for large scale repairs on the engine. Nonetheless, their journey into the outback turned into an unforeseen adventure: On route, the engine started to give them new trouble. Eventually but barely, they made it to Alice Springs where they had it serviced again, only to be told that in Cairns no service had been done at all! Worse: the Alice based garage couldn't do much for them, but promised to come to their help in case of need, bid them farewell and wished them god speed. So they drove on with mostly hope under the hood, but after having made it for another 300 kilometers, the car broke down completely – far away from any settlement. Following that – in the two former car owner's words – the garage owner from Alice was kind enough to live up to his promise, came to pick up them and the car by truck, gave them a lift and levied the worry of what to do with the wreck off their backs by purchasing it for scrap value. So these two continued their journey by public transport on long distance bus passes.

Bus passes are one of the many service offers travellers can purchase as part of packaged deals. Quality of the contents of such packages varies. While major, renowned bus companies and tour operators have a reputation to lose, their services sometimes are sold mixed with offerings of tiny companies set up and out there solely to turn a quick buck. Package deals are on offer everywhere. Especially along the east coast of Queensland (known as the Travel Trail, as it's a route well-liked and oft-visited, foremost by young, travel-unwise and naive backpacker tourists) many cheap deals are available which offer to take visitors close to the most well-known sights (but sometimes only into their general vicinity – which, with Australia's huge distances, can be both comparatively close-by and still a world away). It's a common sight to come across fliers and posters offering packaged deals for the Travel Trail, touting combinations of a couple of nights in hostel accommodation (usually far too few to cover the whole trail) plus tours (such as sailing trips around the Great Barrier Reef or the Whitsundays) at rock bottom prices far below AUD 400 and advertised in places as far away from the Travel Trail as Sydney (which is about 1000 kilometers from the trail's southern end); in other words: In places so far away from where the service delivery would be happening that its impossible to check in person prior to purchase if the packaged offering was good value for money – or at least ask around about it. As I was told, people had made bad experiences with rather low overall quality, unreliable crew and places and ships that were run down and untidy. In case that's what you'll be finding yourself in once you are en route: Could you by then get out or claim an exchange or refund? And could you afford switching to other travel options?

You get what you pay for, don't you? In the case of car buy-back deals that looks to be quite a lot. With such a deal, you purchase a used car along with the promise that the seller buys it back after a set time when you're done with your journey. Those deals are offered by used car dealerships with car repair shops of their own. In detail, they offer you thoroughly checked cars complete with three guarantees: first, the usual warranties required by law; second, the aforementioned promise to buy the car back from you after you completed your journey; and third – and here comes the catch in it – a fixed and guaranteed buy-back price. But that this price is exactly half of the purchase price you'll pay when getting the car for yourself – too bad, because the initial purchase price is sky-high above those on the open market, so when you'll try to sell the car, no one would be ready to offer you more that the car dealers' buy-back price. Thus, you'll have no choice but to sell the car back with a price difference so huge that renting out a car for the entire journey would've been way cheaper. Late one evening, I myself got shown a station wagon by a crestfallen traveller from Switzerland. It was in the very last few hours before his flight left for taking him back home. I were the third person who declined to purchase the car off him – he had it parked already opposite of the dealers' lot in an industrial area after hours and void of people. Pools of shadow were growing all around us, the light was ebbing and the darkness of night was flooding in; low in the sky I could see behind his bent double posture that the sun was going down fast to settle behind the horizon, and his mind was just setting out to keep step with his foreboding, settling into the inevitable.

So make sure that any claims made live up to reality and actually are good ones, not just good sounding ones – for example when you want to remain in contact: Right after arriving to Australia, I went to choose a prepaid mobile phone contract. I equipped myself with offers from Telstra (the national carrier) and Vodafone. Upon comparing those two, the difference was significant: Telstra claimed to have only about 25% coverage, while Vodafone boasted to offer 95%! Since I intended to travel around a lot and be approachable for as much time as possible, I entered into a contract with Vodafone with no further questions asked. When later I had to get a new mobile and prepaid SIM card (see above: backpack and contents stolen in Darwin), I checked offerings anew from these two and other carriers. It turned out that each of them had calculated the statistics each advertised with using wholly different units: Telstra offered a coverage of 25% of the entire land. Vodafone on the contrary was solely referring to populated areas – and of those, they covered only 95%. To really grasp that one must know that in Australia 100% of the population have mustered their housing on only 2% of the land. So Vodafone's coverage was actually about 93% less than that of Telstra! And that explains very well what I had experienced during two car rides through the Outback from Brisbane to Roma. On the first ride, the mobile phone I carried was equipped with a SIM card from Vodafone whereas on the second ride I carried another one connected by Telstra. On the road, left and right of me (as well as in front of and behind me) the ground was carpeted with golden yellow wheat fields up until the faraway horizon. The road always ran contiguously to a train track which solely served to export the crop – non-electrified, single line, lying flat on the bare ground. Every few dozen kilometers or so, the road ran through small settlements, gatherings of narrow nondescript white bungalows with not a single side street interspersed. In each settlement, behind its tiny houses and next to the train track, a grain terminal and two shunting sidings could be descried. And towering over each of these ensembles were the only elements of local skylines, standing like cut-outs against the otherwise uninterrupted forget-me-not-blue sky dome: one to five round silos fabricated from polished sheet steel, much taller than all the local bungalows stacked on each other would've been. Apart from these few, always identical elements, the settlements featured: nothing – expect for traffic signs standing besides the road on the verge of the settlements, announcing that it was forbidden for road trains to use their (incredibly loud) engine breaks for decelerating to intra-urban speed limit. Now, when I was driving on that road my Vodafone-connected mobile phone would lose connection (or even switch to Telstra roaming!) each time I departed a settlement, thus building up an extensive collection of SMS from Telstra with information about roaming and leaving me with a dead battery way before I reached my destination. On the second trip however, Telstra's infrastructure provided me with a connection during the entire all day long journey and subsequently, the battery still had enough energy to keep going for weeks.

Drink spiking

Watch your drink when you're drinking with other people! Because unfortunately it happens frequently that drinks get spiked with (legal and illegal) substances. Some people have died from that, others have had even worse experiences. The danger is so widespread there even are government initiatives to inform and warn the public about this risk. Further, laws have been put into place that make it compulsory for places that sell drinks to inform customers about the risk, and train staff to act as watchdogs. Some of these places even exclusively serve drinks sealed off into tamper-proof containers that are equipped with lids and non-return valves!

Health agency's advice, summarized in short, are: always keep watch over your drink. Pick it up yourself from the bar, even when someone invites you. Notify bar staff immediately if a drink tastes odd or funny, if you feel strange after consuming it or if it makes you more drunk than you expected. If necessary, turn to the nearest hospital's emergency room.

I once stumbled into an event targeted at teenagers, organized by Queensland Health Ministry staff. It took place on the roadside on North Stradbroke Island – they wanted to keep teenagers from getting drunk and into trouble on the lonely, unsupervised and unlit beach; they offered free sports games, pizza and a t-shirt giveaway. To the frustration of the staff I were the sole visitor who stayed longer than just a few moments; a host of teenagers was just passing through, shouting to each other about where to meet on the beach. Eventually after a few minutes of me listening to their stories of disappointment and sharing leftover pizza, I was presented with a T-Shirt. Now whereas neither event nor the message printed onto the T-shirt's front were about drink spiking, on the lower back it carried a subtle warning about drink spiking – as if its makers were intending to repeat it whenever and wherever possible like jetliner crews that perform the world-famous security advice ballet prior to each and every takeoff: "SpikingCanHappen@Anytime.WatchYourDrink".

The first time I saw government-prescribed warnings was on a Saturday night in a bar in Byron Bay There, I had ordered myself a glass of lemonade from the menu. But it looked like nothing I had seen before, and one sip from it revealed a very funny taste. I took a closer look: It was milky white – and on second sip it tasted even funnier – like an artificial flavoring imitating dragon fruit. The words "funny taste" rang a bell and brought to my mind the warnings I had seen on some bulletins just moments ago, so I looked up and around me to re-read them. I were still standing in the exact same spot where I had received that drink. Around me were loads of groups of attendees airily chatting away to each other as if the world was in perfect order. Right next to me stood the bar, behind which the seemingly calm barkeeper (dressed in white shirt and black tie) was going about his work. He had his back to the dark blue and green tiled wall, which was hiding under plenty of warning bulletins that law requires (all of laminated print-outs on white letter paper, written in bold black standard office package typeface). Besides messages that each bar has on display (such as that alcoholic beverages aren't served to people already drunk), there was one asking attendants to notify staff if a drink tasted funny. I took that one verbatim and addressed the barkeeper about my lemonade. He immediately lost his calm, got tense and started to scan the room behind me, asking (without looking at me directly) "Who did you get it from?", apparently keen on finding and expelling the supposed wrongdoer. When I explained that he himself had served the lemonade to me just a mere moment ago (what the issue actually was about), he kindly offered me a replacement, suggesting a freshly drawn beer, but since I prefer non-alcoholics, a short discussion of the menu ensued. Eventually I settled on ordering the sole soft drink the place had in stock apart from lemonade: cold water, straight from the tap – shaken, not stirred.

Confrontational behavior

In the early years of settlement, Australia was even more sparsely populated than it is today. Back then any encounter with a stranger could have been an encounter with an ill-disposed, dangerous person. That's when Australians developed a simple test to gauge personality and attitude of someone they encountered for the first time. The test consists of three easy, short steps: 1.) Curse the person as badly as you can. 2.) Repeat step 1 several times. 3.) Watch how the person reacts after each insult; draw appropriate conclusions and consequences.

This behavior still prevails today – predominantly in social situations when Australians are making new friends (and especially in situations where alcoholic beverages are consumed together). From a visitor's perspective, making the acquaintance of Australians practicing this social behavior looks like the following: Initially, they will be their usual friendly selves. After three or four sentences, they will curse you really badly – entirely out of the blue and unprovoked. But while doing so (and in-between when listening to your reply and observing your reaction), their entire pose, facial expression, gestures and mannerisms will appear relaxed and peaceful to the utmost (every Australian nearby will listen in likewise). Further, the curses they say will be very general against groups that you do or might belong to – not at all meant immediately personally (thus you could only take them personally if you wanted to). Plus, the tone of voice in which they curse is that of a calmly uttered rhetoric question that hangs in the air unfinished and with an open end, looking for being taken up to be proved or disproved. The reaction expected following this behavior is that you do the very same and play your part well in this social exchange: Be peaceful and relaxed, except with the insults you say in return (and only curse groups your counterpart might belong to, not them personally). After this exchange has gone back and forth three or four times, participants and bystanders will beam broadly and happily. They will switch their calm, expectant posture for large friendly gestures and announce to you (speaking loudly so anyone around can take notice) that they consider you to be an alright, good person. Thus, because you've just proven to them your humor, familiarity with Australian social rules and polite manners, from this moment onwards they'll be good pals with you, extend trust towards you and even might let you partake in their habit of mutually buying each other rounds of drinks.

To Germans, cursing others means one is looking for trouble and to provoke a brawl for no reason at all an attitude which clashes head-on with in fact well-meant polite Australian manners. It happened twice that I got to witness this significant difference in understanding of: On both occasions, I were with mixed groups consisting of Germans and Australians that were visiting a pub together; all of them had only recently gotten to know each other and as groups had decided spontaneously to go out for drinks together – obviously intending to get to know each other better. Thus in both groups, the people who were there were quite certainly aiming to show the best of themselves and their manners for making new friends, which led to the following incidents which I had to witness: On both occasions, all group members had sat down moments ago in a pub at a single, long table and gotten served drinks – then one of the Australians present started to do Australian's usual trust-building endeavor. Immediately, all of the Germans present stood up immediately and unanimously without speaking as if the fire alarm had gone off; they downed and fully floored their drinks in the blink of an eye, grabbed coins from their purses then almost thumped the table when laying down the money (thus leaving it to pay without waiting for change, the bill or at least a member of the waitstaff to explain what they were doing), grabbed their belongings and left the pub without giving a single word of explanation – all that happened without them speaking and in less than half a minute. The Australians were baffled and looked at each other amazed and with non-understanding, having expected a wholly different reaction. I however, knowing the customs of both countries, didn't see any reason to leave and, believing they might return, stayed. I understood what those Germans did – and at the same didn't, similar to a Spaniard who was with one of the groups. She shrugged, gazing disappointed at the last German just rushing out over the doorstep. Believing that they might return, I stayed put on both occasions instead of rushing after them to explain, continuing to partake in the exchanges of good Australian manners (which was, you might guess it, cursing back – while trying to not burst into laughter at the absolutely overdone curses those vis-à-vis to me uttered with obviously staged grimness). I thus passed the personality check and subsequently were formally invited and introduced into their circles of good pals. Following that, I were invited to so many round of drinks I weren't able to pay back on the same night and really had a great time. Those other people from Germany however missed out on that entirely. To my amazement, they never ever showed up again, not there in those pubs, not were the groups had initially met or in any other place.

Talking about Australian manners – "How are you?" is Australian for "Hello!" The expected reply is "Good, thanks! How are you?", which will be met with "Good, thanks!" While this small talk may seem to be brief and superficial, it actually serves several serious social purposes: to greet, to initiate contact and (among good acquaintances and friends) it shows one cares deeply. It even can act as a stand-alone, complete social exchange – I got to witness that myself while I waited for eight hours onto a long distance bus insides a rest stop restaurant. Eventually, a travel coach stopped for a break, bringing with it members of a teenage sports team. Several of them interacted like that, obviously glad with these social exchanges. Now, if one would take the opening question literal and answer with an explanation of how one actually was would venture far away from Australian manners that intend to show social greeting, assure each other that one would care and initiate contact – not to seek to find out in detail how one actually is. I met a few people who mistakenly believed Australians were superficial because of their puzzled and irritated looks when they replied with how they actually felt.

Making love
Make sure the only people present are those whom you want to be there. Close and lock all doors and windows and ensure they remain locked.

After several days of major newspapers running headline stories about the misconduct of members of the "Queensland Blue" rugby team, their brand-new ex-major sponsor had commercials aired to angrily express that they had severed all ties with those people.

This ends the section on risks coming at you from other people in general. As said, about 5% of the behavior of the people you meet during travel are different from what you're accustomed to. These 5% can contain risks for you which you're totally unsuspecting of.
Some risks relating to special circumstances will follow soon. Next: more risks coming at you from other people which you're likely to be unsuspecting of.

Hazards – companies and authorities

People form organizations – it's simply in our nature to gather and create formal institutions such as states, authorities, companies and other kinds of communities. It's likely that you'd have to deal with one or the other during your journey. Possibly, unwritten rules or hidden agendas an organization or some of its members might hold may put you at risk or at least in unfavorable circumstances.

Make a conscious effort to make it back home alive and healthy!

Law enforcement

Australian police officers are friendly, resourceful and always eager to serve. Yet what you'll be getting from them could be different from what you had expected. Unruly or unlawful behavior is severely frowned upon, and authorities frequently and eagerly like to "crack down" on criminals as well as against people whose behavior is considered to be antisocial. This is done in the safety of large groups and following the motto of "arrest now, ask later".

It was a late Saturday evening in the Cairns city center – it was a pitch black night but it was as warm as if the sun was still sitting high in the sky. I had only just left a bar hosting a karaoke show even though the show was good, the bar was a comfy place to be and the show only just had started – the reason being that I felt very tired after a full-day trip visiting the Great Barrier Reef. In front of the bar a young woman in good mood addressed me: Whether I'd like to visit that bar with her? But since I were set on my plans to call it a day, my spontaneous reply – without thinking it through – was plain out: No. Upon which something in her suddenly seemed to snap and she started weeping – as surprisingly as a rain shower falling out of the blue. She sat down with me on an adjacent lawn and didn't stop crying as if heavens were going to come crashing down, despite my attempts to console her – this went on for so much time that I lost track of it. Eventually, when she seemed to burp or chuck something up, I came under the impression that possibly she was ill and needed help (or maybe better said: that I needed help helping her). Not knowing how to best take care of her or improve the situation, I contacted police via my mobile phone, asking for her to be put in touch with a women's shelter. From back home I knew these to be safe places where trained specialists were on duty 24/7 to protect and help women. The person who took my emergency call immediately assured me that two guards had been dispatched and were on their way to us; then told me to stay put. So there we were: sitting on a small, brightly lit lawn a few steps away from a pedestrian walkway alongside a road, sitting on drought-resistant, thick-leaved grass through which here and there heads of a permanently installed sprinkler system stuck out, the lawn being surrounded by beds full of drought-resistant plants in muted pastel colors, and in my arms this women – leaning on my shoulder and curled up – and me, holding in my hands each and every single handkerchief I had had with me, meanwhile all of them soaked wet with her tears. After several minutes of nothing happening, a man and a woman dressed in dark blue police uniforms appeared on the walkway in front of us, approaching us swiftly. Without ado or any questions, they pulled the young woman onto her feet and immediately guided her away into the direction from which the two had walked up. I remained behind since the police people had fully ignored me and since I didn't knew what I could contribute. For a moment, I was glad that now she was being taken care of by trained specialist helpers and that I could leave the helping to them and bank on them – because that's how as a kid I had been explained the job of the police: as "to protect and to serve", which in me had grown a huge level of trust and confidence into their intentions and abilities. I were sure – more precisely: I felt I just knew: Now everything would turn out to be alright! I felt so delighted that a moment later I started to curiously imagine and wonder: What would be happening next? Exactly how would she be helped, could I maybe learn some abilities from it? How soon would she start to feel better thanks to the help of the police? To bear in mind the thought of sure help I were

Make a conscious effort to make it back home alive and healthy!

sure she was receiving gladdened me for a moment, then reality started to dawn on me and I continued to ask myself, now doubting: Why had it looked like the police people had jammed her between the two of them and then like they had led her away? Was that a way readily serving protectors were supposed to act – and whom or which purposes were they serving in doing so? I climbed up onto my legs, then walked off the lawn and into the direction where the tiny group had disappeared. I found the three just moments later at the very next street corner insides a parked police car. It was a UTE – sitting on its flatbed back was a tiny locked cage made of white, easily washable plastic. It was into it that the police people had placed the young woman – the cell was so tiny she had to sit crouched. I spoke to her through the bars, trying to cheer her up and console her. Then I addressed the police people sedentary in the front, asking them about their plans. They only spoke to me through a window pulled down by less than an inch, seeming to be frustrated and annoyed – as well as irritated and surprised that I cared about the person in the back and addressed them about that. Their faces remained hidden in the shadow under the roof of the car. I asked them: What were their plans to steer the situation at hand towards a good ending? Their plan was quite simple: Taking the young woman back home – as if to them she just appeared to be drunk and acting antisocial and requiring for them to teach her a lesson by firmly putting her back into place where she belonged: back home, even though that would mean to put her back into circumstances she had tried to leave behind her. Conclusion, in short: If you ask for help you might not always get what you hope for. If you can make do on your own that might be a better idea.

Overstepping the law is handled strictly with tough measures when caught. One such law especially affecting travellers is visa regulation. Overstaying visas (or working longer than a work permit allows) is punished with long-term eviction from the country. Thus, anyone wishing to stay longer should make that decision well in advance to have sufficient time to inform the authorities and timely hand in the forms required. News about large-scale coordinated crack downs report how authorities have stopped cars in areas where many foreign visitors work, searched these as well as workplaces, checked peoples' paperwork, arrested and jailed those without a sufficient permit and finally thrown them out of the country.

Are you sure you're insured?
It seems like a good idea to get insurance that covers your travel, such as for your health or for equipment you take with you or rent out. However, making claims on it may be difficult.

There's a one-man company which since decades ago recurrently organizes tours of the Canning Stock Route – an outback track famous for its ruggedness and remoteness from any civilized infrastructure that's only drivable by 4WD vehicles and part of which crosses the Great Sandy Desert. That company puts together 20-cars strong convoys with each vehicle being rented out to participants (including full damage insurance cover). It takes each tour group two full weeks to drive from Perth through remote areas to Darwin, passing on the way through few settlements and plenty of landscape. The reason why I'm mentioning this company here is a sentence mentioned in their marketing material targeted at participants from Germany: Based on their decades of experience, it advises them to get additional cover from a certain German insurance company. The point to note about that hint lies in the nature of that company: They only underwrite one type of risk: legal costs.

How might that piece of advice have come to be? My guess: A few insurance companies have earned themselves a bad reputation through unduly critical appraisals of claims and by outright rejections even of fully legitimate claims. Reports have it that claimants had to take them to court to have an independent third party confirm their claim and entitle them to enforce it. But even if you would go that route and win, the insurance company may try and find a way to wiggle out of it. I myself took out health and luggage insurance and once had a case for a claim. But it never happened that I even got around to lodge the claim, because it turned out to be too difficult to contact the insurance company for clarification of whether or not that case was covered. I hadn't anticipated such issues – quite to the contrary, because I had entered into an insurance contract with a well-known, reputable and decades-old German underwriter. I considered lodging a claim with them after having gotten hurt – I had been enjoying breakfast one morning on a sandy Tasmanian beach and during that had tilted over upon sitting down into a camping chair that sank into the soft sand, so that I bumped into a metal pole which had been standing next to my chair. My side was hurting for days on end. Finally, I went to see a doctor about it. There, at the office's door I were welcomed by an assistant and invited in. I did a step forward, then spontaneously halted in mid-air to ask what was bothering me about as much as the injury: Would my insurance cover the treatment? The assistant replied with a perplexed look on her face: The sole point of contact able to give me definite yes or noes would be the insurance company itself. So I said my goodbye to check before returning for a treatment (which eventually never came to be; despite the assistants cordial invitation upon my departure) and left to call the insurance company. When looking for their contact data, for the first time ever I read our contract in its entirety. To my surprise it revealed that in addition to their headquarter located in Germany (a palace-like office building which I once had toured in person), they operated numerous offices distributed across the world, sharing regional responsibilities. Their headquarters solely dealt with cases that arose within Europe. Claims that arose within the Asia-Pacific region and Oceania were dealt with by their US-based office – about ten time zones or many country borders and half a world away from where I was located. Imagine the effort I would've needed to exert in order to take them to court in case I would've had to. However, my case never made it anywhere even remotely in shouting distance of that. What followed – but lead to nowhere and nothing – was that over the course of the next several following days I attempted to reach their US crew by phone in order to clarify if this damage actually was covered and if so, how I might claim back costs of treatment which might accrue. But anytime I rang them up, no one picked up – not even during office hours – the tune of the phone ringing eventually took up to follow me around, reminding me of the unaccomplished task, until eventually I could sing along to it synchronously when making what I knew was going to be just another fruitless call. After a couple of days during which I didn't got any closer to my goal I additionally sent them my questions by email – which I had to follow up a few times until eventually I received a reply from a real person. However, members of that company ignored half of my questions and answered the remaining ones with elusive, incomplete sentences – even numerous further emails I sent for clarification were treated like that; and that wasn't due to any incorrect interpretations triggered by my language skills the wording I used – I actually used plain yes-no questions to make myself easy and unmistakeable to understand (which native speakers confirmed whom to make sure I had asked to countercheck my emails). Further, to prevent the case that staff members of the insurance company would not understand my emails in part or in full, I always closed them with the common phrase that I was available for clarification if any parts of my messages were not understandable. However, they never asked. Summarizing: Quite obviously they did not wanted to confirm that this case was covered and that they would have been liable to cover any treatment costs caused by it. Eventually after several days, my futile attempts to attain that confirmation had taken so much time that in the meantime I had bettered without any outside help or treatment – much to my joy and relief on the one hand, but on the other about as much to my disappointment about the insurance that had turned out to be nothing but a broken umbrella which had left me standing in the rain at the very moment it had started to pour down.

By the way: That same insurance policy expressively precluded any and all damages arising from "dangerous activities of any kind". The paragraph referring to this contained a non-exhaustive list of examples for these. It included hiking, which was a very limiting exclusion, because: Could you really see and experience Australia without taking at least one stroll in one of the many national parks, where each and ever walkway is called a hiking path? In case you'd be offered a hike together by friends, acquaintances or a travel group, would you stay behind alone and forgo the shared experience? "Great hikes of Australia" isn't merely a marketing label for some Australian hiking paths but a reality on most of them. Thus it didn't came as a surprise that it was in Australia that I first heard the saying "You've only really been to places you've been to on feet." Telling from my own experience on hours-long hikes through unsettled, seemingly untouched wilderness that's true. And I'm not the first one to find out as I learned by coincidence – that saying is actually a quote from a well-known, widely published traveller: Johann Wolfgang von Goethe.

Limitations for coverage exist for car insurances as well. Some of them are only valid as long as a car has tarmac under all of its wheels. However, it's easy to find unpaved roads consisting of only gravel or sand, or corrugated roads consisting of nothing but smoothed soil. I can list many examples just off the top of my head: inner-city streets, approach roads to national parks or homes outback and even major intercity highway routes. If you did encounter such a piece of road, would you make a detour to find and stick to tarmac at all means? In some cases, that would require you to go a long way round for several hundreds of kilometers – provided that such a way existed at all.

Employers

Which kind of work is offered most frequently to travellers on Working-Holiday-Visas that are searching for an employment? It's mostly only casual work, meaning: low-paid and unqualified work. This is caused by a barrier built into this kind of visas: Three month are the maximum length of time one is allowed to stay with any single employer. This makes extensive familiarization a wasted effort to any employer – and qualified, well-paid work always requires a familiarization. Plus, holders of this type of visa commonly don't yet have undergone formal job training towards qualifications that employers demand for only three months. Unfortunately all of this severely limits the choices available to and weakens the bargaining power of travellers – unfortunately there are criminals

Make a conscious effort to make it back home alive and healthy!

pretending to be employers which abuse this situation to their own advantage, shielded by the facts that public authorities and the press only act when alarmed, that worker's unions fight for their members first (and only when alarmed), that a lot of casual work takes place in settlements or on farms remote from any authorities that might prevent this if they conducted regular checks as they're supposed to, that foreigners are encouraged to come travel and work in Australia but are not educated about their worker's rights. This has encouraged some employers to habitually forget about the law or even to actively abuse the situation and turn criminal.

Four acquaintances of me had been employed a plant where freshly picked bananas were washed and packed. No protective gloves were provided. Thus, everybody working there pulled the fruit through the washing water bare-handed. However, since fruit usually are doused with toxic chemicals during their growth, the process of washing was supposed to get the chemicals off before putting the fruit into customer's hands and thus the washing water was nothing but a toxic cocktail, causing my acquaintances and the other workers severe rashes requiring medical attendance.

But even an employer does provide safety gear there are some employees who don't use it with no foreperson or employer bothering to order them to properly protect themselves – as if these believed that by providing, but not explaining the gear their obligations as caring employers were already fulfilled. The outcome of that? I once visited friends from home who worked at a factory packed with machinery in motion 24/7 that emitted deafening noise despite catering to a simple task solely: picking brochures of piles one after the other, then mixing and packing them into envelopes. My friends were part of a machine operating crew featuring mostly local employees. The latter were chatting away happily all day long over the noise, even listening the music blasting from a radio over the loud machine noise. My friends in contrast to that showed quite a different behavior: They had chosen to forfeit both listening to music and chatting with colleagues while working, to remain closemouthed during their entire working days and to talk (if at all) with gestures only. In fact, they couldn't talk any way else while working because, different from the locals, they had opted to protect their hearing by wearing the earplugs the employer provided. The reason for that remained a puzzling mystery to the locals. Only when during one lunch break one of them started to wonder and think why the visiting workers did that did he grasped there was a cause and reason why his own ears were ringing and his hearing was impaired after a regular working day filled with constant machine noise working on the ruination of unprotected worker's hearing.

Besides protective gear, experience may help you stay safe. Prerequisite to that however is: You got it or you know and listen to someone who does. When volunteering at some horse stables, I handled horses for the first time in my life. I found them to be very comparable to two-year-olds. Every single one has a distinct character and they all act very impulsively; in mere fractions of a second, their moods would shift and their ranges emotions they can run through in under a minute encompasses all of friendliness, calmness, playful curiosity, feeling of security, affection, shy reservation, fear, gluttony, wrath, headless panic, gluttony and raging anger. But while an enraged small child may only take to the ground, scream ear-piercingly and feebly throw small objects, foals and horses are empowered by four long, muscle-laden legs (one on each corner so they can reach out 360° into the entire area surrounding them) and in addition have a built-in reaction the flee to the fore on any (presumed) danger while at the same time kicking to the rear. Now those kicks really can be dangerous: Horses' legs are so strong they can punch a fist-deep hole into a solid wall with just one kick! During my time on the farm, I got to witness that myself on several occasions – got to see how all the workers stood silent for a moment (eyes wide and tight-lipped) looking openly or hesitantly from the corners of their eyes at each other to check if everybody else was fine while around us the echoes of the bangs were subsiding slowly (yet faster than the ones insides our heads), while the clouds of dust that had been kicked up where hovering for endless minutes in the golden beams of sunlight that was filtering in from dawn until dusk through all the openings; and I got to encounter the layers of stone turned into dust while sweeping the stables – the dust had mixed on the ground with hay and trampled earth and shriveled lupine dropped from the throughs into a melange which was as heavy as solid bricks. Luckily, my horse-experienced colleagues had taught me at the very outset of my engagement how to lower the risk of getting kicked while passing a horse with little clearance. But what if they hadn't taught me? I would've never figured out that I were exposing myself to danger, not to mention how to handle it!

The press has frequently gotten wind of how travellers as employees are deliberately maltreated and put into danger. Take for example the numerous operators of Working Hostels (hostels that place workers). Worker's unions estimate that about a third of them systematically abuses traveller's fragile situation to their own advantage. Cause of this fragility are: lack of knowledge of the local language, not knowing about legal rights, coming from a culture of obedience and/or desperately seeking for an employment in agriculture in a remote area (as having completed such is a prerequisite when applying for an extension of a working holiday visa). Below I list what criminal work placement agents or Working Hostel operators have done to the innocent (according to reports verified by union representatives and the media), so that you'll be able to better recognize if you or others receive bad, unlawful treatment:

- demanding (usually horrendously high) fees and deposits as prerequisite for closing contracts – and later blackmailing with the threat to keep these
- tie placement into work to the purchase of additional (overpriced and entirely superfluous) services – and threaten to immediately terminate contracts if usage of these services is rejected
- provide solely run-down, crammed accommodation with extremely bad fittings
- pay far less than the minimum wage required by law
- pay by work completed – instead, as prescribed by law, per time worked
- prior to signing a contract, pretend that work was available immediately, and only inform after the contract was closed (and fees and deposits were paid) that this statement didn't accurately describe the current situation (that is: it was a deliberate lie), then giving solely guesses as to when work (and thus opportunities to earn an income and cover the cost of lodging at the Working Hostel) might become available
- ignore legal obligations to protect employees (such as worker's rights to breaks and to protection from UV radiation and heat)
- offer unpaid "volunteer" work without owning an official permit to do so

- threaten travellers (personally or with alleged easy replaceability of lowly educated workers), shout at, molest or otherwise damage them

Travel agents

Do you know how travel agents earn their income? They live off selling you tours, transports and accommodation – the more the better for them! Thus they have an inclination to tell you anything necessary to talk you into the purchase of flights, guided tours, hotels and excursions. Sadly, that includes questionable methods. I've witnessed some agents telling half-truths, keeping information from me, refraining from correcting my erroneous assumptions and skipping directing me to cheaper offerings. In short: They might promise aplenty and deliver a little. Quite unfortunate, because what they sell you impacts your experience and your future memories. Actually, travel agents should inform correctly and thoroughly to ensure you only make good memories. But apparently some couldn't care less. And why should they – do they have anything to fear? Once you've paid, the money is theirs to keep, and once you're out the door and departed to venture out (as a traveller on a long journey) you're not likely to return to a place you've already been to and checked off your list. To them, this limits the risk that you'd ever return to complain even if you wanted to – and that makes it quite likely that (if at all) you'd blame bad experiences solely on yourself or other circumstances, not on a travel agent who sold you down the river.

"We know because we go" – with this claim each travel agent I spoke to wooed for my trust. Turned out they rather didn't. Some didn't even know their own neighborhood, and some deliberately misinformed. Upon my first days in Australia, I got to attend a presentation on the country held by a travel agent; he was the first person from which I'd heard said claim. He went on to warn his audience about the extent of distances between cities and sights. According to him, driving a car by yourself through remote Australia was dreary and no fun at – he recommended to us that rather we should book and go on a guided group tour (with which he'd gladly assist us). After a few weeks with guided tours eating away at my savings, I opted to go by car and I took to the road either with friends in shared cars or by myself, venturing out in rental cars. Turned out that driving through Australia actually is a great experience: It takes you to marvelous places to which tours don't go – all that and following your own, completely flexible itinerary. On top of that it makes for a much closer, impressive and intensive experience of the vast landscape – anytime when a traveller was aboard with me who got to experience the outback for the first time, the very first moment (to them) that we crossed a bend in the road and faced a stretch of tarmac spread out straight ahead until the faraway horizon as if drawn with a very long ruler, they couldn't help but beg us to stop the car, jump out and capture that experience in photos.

Now, even information given wrong without intention can cause confusion and lost effort. Great Keppel Island is a beach-lined tropical islands about 18 kilometers from the mainland coast. I arrived at its youth hostel's reception together with several other guests – we had all been on the same ferry. Its reception desk was positioned outsides among palm trees, due to the constantly fine weather. There, the owner explained to us resort and island. Upon finishing, she demanded if we had any further questions. One guest did and apparently took her by surprise with a presumably unusual requirement: mobile phone reception. How good was it

Make a conscious effort to make it back home alive and healthy!

on the island? Her reply was a simple: No idea – but she remembered that very frequently she had seen people strutting up and down the waterfront promenade on the island's side that was closest to the mainland, while all the while they were constantly looking at their mobile phones. She nodded over to said promenade – a 150 meter long and roughly 1,5 meter wide walkway made of asphalt and wooden beams. Thus, when a few days later I needed to make a phone call (this was in the days before the widespread adoption of smartphones and online social networks), I fetched my mobile phone from my room, turned it on, walked past reception on the way out of the hostel, stood on the boardwalk (briefly scanning the faraway mainland coastline that was almost gulped by the horizon), dialed, then held the phone to my ear and heard: silence. Nothing happened, there wasn't even at least a dial tone! Checking the display revealed the cause: My mobile simply had no network reception in the spot where I was standing (only later did I realize that I were in on an island with limited network coverage). In response, I made a few steps along the boardwalk and checked again. Still no reception. I walked a few steps further and further and checked – and further and checked and eventually I was stilting along the promenade at low pace while constantly looking at my mobile phone in order to capture the second when it would connect so I could freeze into place on the spot and hold on to that connection. While walking, from the corners of my eyes I noticed other pedestrians coming up and dodging me elegantly, some at the very last moment. Some of them were likewise taking a walk with their phones in front of their eyes instead at their ears. When finally on my phone's display the indicator appeared that it had successfully managed to connect, I stopped as if rooted into place and didn't move an inch from there until I had successful completed my call.

Afterwards, thinking of other visitors to the island, I went to search for a piece of chalk in order to mark the spot for them, however I found no such thing. Thus, during the following days, I lived to see how people stilted up and down the waterfront promenade, all the while constantly looking at their mobile phones in front of their eyes fixed instead of holding them to their ears, in search of reception.

In case you consider opting for an organized group tour as means of travel: Tours differ from each other significantly in content, even if their published and advertised itineraries and lists of sights covered appear nearly identical. Now, when visited Uluru as member of a group tour, by chance I got to observe travellers on another one; so here's a comparison of differences in seemingly identical tour itineraries that I got to observe on site: Early one morning, we were standing in the vantage site for watching the rising sun shine on Uluru. We had our feet in the reddish sand and got to enjoy in calm how the colorful display changed from moment to moment. Some time during that, I took notice of another tour group. The tour bus they were on was rushing into the parking lot belatedly – the sunrise already was in full motion and for quite some time there hadn't been any new arrivals to the vantage site. Their tour guide shooed them out of the bus, then hectically loaded them with their (heavy and large) backpacks from the buses' luggage compartment and finally lead them off onto a hike past Uluru – or said more fittingly: spurring them onwards like a dog driving a sheepflock. Presumably, that was supposed to be a hike at Uluru at sunrise – such are touted as part of pretty much any tour that visits this sight. However, it's quite a difference if a hike is "at" Uluru or "around" it and whether it is "during" or "after" sunrise! Similar (albeit only in general terms) to the group I had seen, my tour group got to enjoy a hike, too.

Make a conscious effort to make it back home alive and healthy!

But ours only commenced after we'd had sufficient time to enjoy the sunrise in full. And: Our itinerary permitted for enough time to complete the circle around the entire of Uluru. Not a single bit of our luggage was laden on our backs (it stayed put in our tour bus which scooped us up afterwards). During the hike (while I ambled onwards at a speed of my own choice, to my left the red rock and to my right the shrub-strewn plain stretching until the horizon, dotted here and there with spots of shadows from tall eucalyptus trees with bark about as white as birch trees), the group of hikers I had noticed earlier was nowhere to be seen. The path they had taken remet the road after running past about a quarter of Uluru, so perhaps they had reboarded their tour bus after having gotten to see only a bit. Apparently, they had been on one of those rather cheap tours which usually sport a very tight itinerary, so they must've already ventured on.

Early during my visit to Australia, I heard about hot springs in Moree. My map showed this town to lie close to Washpool National Park, so I (erroneously) assumed that this would be where the hot springs were. A travel agent took advantage of that erroneous assumption and instead of correcting it sold me his staple product – a bus ticket. With that I managed to make it to Moree, but not to said national park. In Moree, it turned out that the hot springs were actually situated within the Moree city limits and were not a remarkable sight at all. What I found were (since back then upgraded) facilities consisting of two small swimming pools set in a public bath that looked like it already had been plain, pragmatic and undecorated when it had been erected about decades ago in color choices fashionable during those days and area (mostly khaki and mud-brown); the sole nod to decoration being a small art deco statue topping a small waterspout fountain in front of the entrance which lavishly spilled out some of the hot bore water that's so abundant here. As for the pools: the hot springs simply fed into these pools and kept them steaming, with bathers (including me) gladly ignoring the large enamel signs attached to each of the walls round the pools which advised us to limit our time in the water for worry over what length of exposition to the heat our bodies could stand. I remained nonplussed as to why bother going that place (whereas other visitors from Latin America explained to me their rock-solid persuasion that it's in fact worth going due to the positive health effects of the mineral-rich water). Yet as for getting to my initial goal: At the Moree tourist office, I found out that Washpool National Park was still a few hundred kilometers further afield and no scheduled buses went there. Because bus services only connect cities (which are few and sparse, transporting the people living there), not national parks or other sights located outsides of towns (driving to those takes so long that Australians travel there only on self-organized multi-day trips only, usually driving in their own car and bringing their own supplies to be fully self-sufficient). It was there in Moree that I realized that places in Australia might look like they were close to each other on a map but in reality (because of its scale and the size of the continent) are far from each other. Therefore, better prepare yourself a plan before you start your journey, so that you won't arrive in a place only to find that your actual goal is someplace else completely.

Logging companies vs. environmental activists
Should you wish to campaign yourself for good causes, secure yourself against those who might perceive you're standing in their way towards their aims.

When I visited a forest on Tasmania whose trees were occupied by activists, I was told about a similar place in another Australian state. There, employees of logging companies had confronted environmental activists, accusing them of damaging their source of income and self-support. The peacefully protesting activists suddenly had to put up with a violent attack. The workers apparently felt safe from prosecution as Australian forests are (as are many places in Australia) remote from authorities or potential third-party witnesses.

Stage diving / crowdsurfing
Australians still tell each other excitedly about a (to them) legendary experience that occurred at a concert by the music band Rammstein on Bondi Beach. The part of their show which has everybody still talking years later (including both among throngs of people who only heard about it and among people who've been there and have seen it themselves) simply was: stage diving. Australians neither know nor do that. That was years ago, but still today stage diving (ideally done securely, people-friendly and with prior notice of the crowd) has not become part of Australian concert culture. So just leave it be – several visitors from abroad attempting that in Australia have gotten hurt upon letting themselves falling from the stage, erroneously assuming that the audience would be in the know and catch them.

It was in a Sydney music club where I gained direct experiences myself of how to Australians react to someone's attempts to stage dive: During the performance of a band, I spontaneously climbed on stage, turned round to face the crowd, leaned forward to let myself fall with straightened body and face towards the audience. But the people towards which I was falling didn't raise their hands to catch and carry me. Instead, they held their hands close to their sides and stepped asides to free the way for me! A large gap in the crowd opened before me, and while I was falling past the audience members I noticed their graciously smiling faces (with an air of admiration as if they believed I had had legitimate business to do on stage and were simply descending after completing a task) and then I only saw the carpet floor rushing up fast towards me. I caught myself in time – different from other visitors from abroad whose nights out ended in hospitals.

This ends the section on some of the risks coming at you from people that you encounter as groups or other social institutions. (By the way: Want to get a satellite-like view in person of the multitude and magnitude of outcomes possible from gathering in groups? Keep an eye out for termite mounds in the Northern Territory.) Up until now I haven't spoken of the risks you typically hear about that exist in Australia. What about them? What about animals?

Hazards – animals

Finally, here's the section that will tell about the dangers that are typical to Australia according to clichés: animals. This encompasses those animals about which (and the dangers they pose) you certainly have heard about before. I'm however starting with those you wouldn't suspect: the ones that look cute and harmless but in reality are very dangerous to deal with.

Kangaroos, wallaroos, wallabies and pademelons
They're present everywhere – even in places where you wouldn't expect them (more on that in the section on getting around by car). And they're strong and sturdy, despite their slim, petite looks.

Make a conscious effort to make it back home alive and healthy!

Kangaroos are boxers – at least, that's how male kangaroo's way of fighting each other is colloquially referred to. Depending on your type of humor, such a fight might look either inefficient or rather funny, because roos only sport twig-thin forearms with hands the same size as those of of a toddler. With that, all punches they could obviously ever do are mild slaps. As I was told, that mislead a Pommie to provoke a roo to fight and box with him. Now, while this urban legend shows the almost cliché prejudices against Britons of the Australian who told it to me, it does contain an important warning – because actually roos do not aim to punch their opponents. Instead, they want to hug them! Because what they really try to do is to put their arms around their opponent's throat and hold on to them in order to push their actual intentions! In case you ever find yourself in a similar situation: Don't let an enraged animal hug and hold on to you – especially not one equipped with strong hind legs that knows how to jump all over – you.

Koala bears

In reality, the cute and harmless looking Koalas are even more cuddly and slow-moving than they appear to be in TV documentations. And they emit an intensive, calming smell of eucalyptus oil, because for their choice of food they are fully content with eating leaves only off this kind of tree. But – did you took note of how tough eucalyptus leaves are? And how massive Koalas' jaws are under all that cuddly fur? They've got the teeth and muscles to chew sufficiently many of those leaves all day long to survive well on this nutrition. With these teeth they can bite to defend themselves – and since eucalyptus leaves are so sturdy, they can bite very hard. Which they might do if they think it's necessary, and surprisingly quick without prior warning – and without you seeing it coming, having been calmed and led to err by all the cuddly fur and slow movements. (These warnings you just read are actually pieced together from improvised warning signs that have been put up in Brisbane and Blue Mountain zoos; they even have hand-drawn icons to warn non-English speakers.)

Box jellyfishes, also known as sea wasp, and other jellyfishes – also known as marine stingers

Poisonous jellyfishes breed north of Australia and migrate south with the sea currents during the warm season. They've even been spotted as far south as Sydney and Perth. Box jellyfishes have several meters long tentacles that contain stinging cells with which they jab and inject deadly poison into any living being accidentally touching it. They're not the only jellyfishes around – they share the waters with incredibly tiny and much more lethal jellyfishes such as the Irukandji jellyfish, the blue bottle or the lion's mane jellyfish.

 A saying recommends: "When in Rome, do like the Romans" – it's a good idea to imitate the local habits since the residents created them for good reasons, even if these are unknown and non-obvious to you and even if their behaviour may at first seem illogical and odd to you. In north-eastern Australia, beach life looks quite uncommon: In Cairns and other cities, pool areas have been edified directly between beaches and ocean forefront promenades. They're unfenced and publicly accessible around the clock – for free (as otherwise only the ocean itself is). People use these pools to mingle, splash and bathe. Nobody ventures onto the adjacent sand to even dip as much as a toe into the ocean.

 Further south down the coast, netted enclosures can be found in the ocean in front of some beaches (which commonly are close to tourist resorts). These are made

Make a conscious effort to make it back home alive and healthy!

of silicone nets on wooden frames kept afloat at the water's surface by buoys. They've been built with the aim of letting water in and keeping jellyfishes out in order to facilitate risk-free swimming (or rather: splashing, as even the largest enclosures are only a couple meters small). In reality however, these enclosures are useless – they can't keep jellyfish out. All the locals I spoke to about them just shook their heads, calling them desperate and fruitless attempts or went straight to recount their concerns to me – with fright in their eyes and tenseness of unease in their postures. Box jellyfish in total may be larger than the meshes, but they very frequently loose tentacles as these rip off easily. Those wee bits fit through the mesh like glass shards trough a door left ajar. Those to whom this isn't enough proof that the enclosures aren't able to provide protection should survey more closely their upper ends: Their upper rim is kept at the surface by buoys – but only "at", not "above" or at least "on". Every wave, as tiny as it might be, washes over the frame and brings into the enclosure whatever it carries with it at that moment. Then, that will remain inside the enclosure – because after arriving into it thanks to a wave, it cannot easily get out again as the net stands in its way.

Another attempt to dodge being stung is just as ill-fated as the enclosures: stinger suits. You can frequently find them for purchase at souvenir shops; their packaging always shows pictures of happily beaming people in bathing attire over which they're wearing those suits made of black webbing (covering almost the entire body). Could these keep you safe from jellyfish? I won't say so. When I visited the Whitsunday Islands on a sailing boat trip, at each stop almost everyone enjoyed taking a bath in the tropical warm water – all the passengers and the captain of the ship (him being the sole crew member in the water). The remainder of the crew (who frequently called the captain crazy, even within his earshot – to which he never reacted or at least raised an eyebrow) shied the water like the plague. One of the crew members (actually the first officer – who said about himself that despite his decades of experience he hadn't any career ambitions to become captain because he wasn't crazy enough to voluntarily take on such an immense amount of responsibility) gravely informed me these suits only made you believe you were in safety. As proof, he told me of a visitor from Asia who was touched and stunned by a tentacle even though he was wearing a stringer suit – it had hit him exactly on the little bit of skin left uncovered by the opening for the mouth.

How dangerous are these box jellyfish anyways? An explanation can be found at Townsville aquarium. It sports an extensive exhibition on animal life in the Great Barrier Reef with many live displays. A preserved box jellyfish can be found there on display, mounted in a frame and hung on a wall. Its tentacles are about six meters long. Below it hangs a picture to illustrate the damage that one of them can cause. It's a large, blown-up photo of a person who's gotten stung. Close-up (and almost completely filling the picture) is a male torso covered with a couple of red marks here and there. In case this sounds harmless: Looking closely at the borders of the picture reveals that person's whereabouts – lying on a stretcher besides an ambulance, with infusion needles stuck into the crooks of his arms and four people in paramedic's uniforms standing next to him. Lucky for him that medical help was close enough to arrive in time to save his life.

The damage and risk from marine stingers is bad enough to encourage authorities along the east coast to put up huge warning signs. Some of them are elaborately designed, several meter high sculptures. Most of them –

even the most modest, rusty signposts – are equipped with boxes that stock white vinegar. That liquid is the only working solution to reduce the risk of even more stings from box and Irukandji jellyfishes, as dousing unreleased stinging cells with it keeps them from firing.

I spotted these warning signs in populated places, such as beach-facing forefronts of towns lying immediately adjacent to the sea. Yet the risk to get attacked and stung by jellyfish exists everywhere in the sea – even where there are no warning signs and no provisions of white vinegar – at beaches close to cities as well as at the many remote beaches along entirely unsettled coastlines (there are many of those in Australia). The risk is ever-present and well-known to locals. They've grown so accustomed to the risk that they believe it to be common knowledge. They thus won't bother to expressively warn you in advance, even when they're with you in the danger zone. I realized that on a stop while sailing around the Whitsunday Islands. Us tourists on this ship tour had already spent half a day with bathing and snorkeling, when I returned aboard for a break. I came across the first officer and in the ensuing small talk mentioned how I was looking forward to go back into the water and enjoy some more snorkeling. At that, he looked me up and down (I was wearing what I deemed to be apt attire for bathing there: swimming trunks) and all of a sudden he turned tense. Then – for a sheer minute – he seemed to fight an inner conflict between disbelief, doubt, sense of responsibility and concern. Finally he burst out, with conscientiousness and worry in his voice: "For heavens' sake, at least put on a T-shirt!". He went on to explain to me that there are poisonous jellyfish even in the waters close to shore and sheltered from the open ocean by the Great Barrier Reef. Not even the reef can keep them away. Locals believe that you know the risk.

Tasmanian devils

Tasmanian devils fight opponents ferociously, commonly hurting (and getting hurt by) members of the same species badly because (compared to total body weight) they're the species of land-based raptors that can bite the hardest. Sadly, that can transfer a virus that causes lethal cancer, which is said to be harmless for humans, but then it's so dangerous Tasmanian devils are in danger of becoming extinct. Good thing they usually keep their distance from humans.

Tasmanian devils prefer to feed on carrion if they find some – which they easily do thanks to their superior sense of smell. On the Australian mainland, when driving on intercity roads one frequently passes by the sorry sight of deceased animals that fell victim to accidents. Along Tasmanian roads however there's not a single carcass to be seen, thanks to the inhabitants: Next to every road large signs announce which local group voluntarily keeps it tidy – good deeds considering that Tasmanian devils have caused car crashes while feeding on carcasses lying in the road.

Sharks

Yes, there are sharks in the ocean. A select few of them have mouths wide enough to damage a human. But even if this limits the risk of being bitten, it's advisable to consider if one would bath in the same waters through which sharks that are dangerous to humans might pass. According to animal encyclopedia, these regions are (depending on the species) the northern coastal waters from Perth to Sydney, as well as the southern coastal waters from Townsville to Carnarvon in Western Australia – in brief: They can be everywhere.

Just off Bondi Beach, enraged visitors have pulled out a shark out of the shallow, ankle-deep water and then killed it – even though it wasn't posing any threat to them; it was less than a meter and its mouth was only wide enough for small fish the diameter of a grissini.

Stingrays

The syllable to note in their name is sting. Reminds you of a rather harmless bee or wasp? It's much worse than that. Stingrays are equipped with a poison sting that sits at the end of a long, muscular tail. If they perceive they were in danger, they stab without giving prior notice. If a sting doesn't get treated within a few minutes, their venom kills the cells around the entry point. Since most Australian beaches are faraway from any civilized infrastructure, you're unlikely to make it to the next hospital alive at all. The consequences differ considerably depending on which part of your body got hit. Stingrays won't make a choice as to that – they have barely any control over their tail when defending themselves as they just whip it over their heads backwards at their victim while escaping forwards. If they hit a leg or an arm perhaps only an amputation will be necessary – that is, if the stingray has stung once only and damaged little. However, commonly stingrays hit both strong and several times. If an organ such as heart of lung is hit, or if the stings cut several bleeding wounds, you'd be left with only enough time to say your farewells. Hopefully, there's someone out there in the water and listening to you to convey your last words.

Steve Irwin attained world fame trough the "Crocodile Hunter" TV series for which he stood in front of the camera with dangerous animals. To film for a new series about dangerous marine animals, he once went out onto the ocean in a rubber boat in order to, search for them. In the boat with him was his cameraman, a friend of 15 years. They encountered a very large specimen (the largest species of stingrays lodge around Australia) and got in the water for close-up filming. When Steve swam closer to the stingray, it hit him without advance warning. The prime ministers of Australia and of Queensland offered to his family to give him a state funeral, but they turned it down, explaining that Steve had been just a regular Australian bloke.

Spiders

Most of the world's species of poisonous spiders live on the Australian continent. Many of them are huge, but the most poisonous are rather tiny. Keep your distance.

It was a sunny day on Tasmania. The sky was a perfect spotless blue that arched above us from one horizon to the other. The air had a springtime mildness to it and I was travelling with two acquaintances from Switzerland: two women who had been working together as colleagues and in doing so became friends. It was our first day on Tasmania; the evening before, we had arrived on the ferry from Melbourne; just when we had been driving off the ferry and out of Davenport in the camper-van the two owned, the sun had been disappearing behind the horizon with a colorful light show. A short distance away from the town, we then had camped and cooked. That had taken us until late and we carelessly had left the doors standing wide open. The next morning, we had enjoyed breakfast, then I had dismantled my tent and we had driven off. The camper van was equipped with a single bench at the front, so there we three sat all in a row, me being seated right next to one of the doors. We drove for a few hours when all of a sudden – the very moment in which we were traversing over an intersection – a huge spider the size of a dinner plate came crawling from under the folded-up sun visor above the driver's seat! It had a black corpus the size of an orange, walked on long, light gray legs as thin as sticks and was overall very hairy. The two women immediately started to shriek loudly at the top of their lungs, jumped out and in doing so bumped me out of the way and the car as well. They ran about the place, continuing to shriek piercingly. So there I was, standing on the open road in the middle of an intersection, wondering how I ever might get the spider out and calm down the constantly screeching women. That moment, my eyes fell on the camper-van. It was still rolling forward, albeit a slow speed; further I grasped what showed itself quite plainly in front of me: around us on the road were three other cars waiting to enter and pass the intersection, too – we were blocking their way and putting them at risk depending on where the camper-van would be trundling. In the background, behind the cars, I noted a small green hill – one of the three roads came down from it. Above my head was the blue sky and below was pitch black asphalt with painted yellow lines, bordered by guard rails. All these impressions pressed on me in a single moment. The next moment, I witnessed how the two women – still screeching – rushed back to the front of the van with improvised tools they obviously had gathered from the luggage compartment while I had been standing around planless, wiped the spider out of the door and then jumped back in and seated themselves. I jumped right after them as I didn't wanted to stay behind alone. Immediately, we slam shut the doors, the two stopped to scream (like sirens turned off – the sudden silence sounded like thunder turned inside out) and we drove on as if nothing had happened. Lesson learned: women can be more calm, focused and solution-oriented than men, even if at first impression it appears the other way around.

As I found out later, that jaywalking animal had been a huntsman spider. Members of this species use to wander around in search of prey, frequently stationing themselves in houses, huts, garages and cars – about anyplace where they can find an opening to enter through. Comparable habits are exhibited by other spiders, including the very toxic and well-known redback spider. That species is so famous that a few years ago when Australia Post released a series of stamps depicting Australia's most dangerous animals, they had a draft created that does show a redback spider. However, since these spiders frequently nest in manmade yet rarely disturbed objects, that stamp was never released to the public to guard against that recipients would get shocked and scared from checking their mailbox and mistakenly believing they were encountering an actual poisonous spider.

Snakes and scorpions

These tiny critters like to hide and some of them are hard to see thanks to their great camouflage. Some species are almost completely transparent. They're not picky as to where to hide; they lodge everyplace they can squeeze in themselves. So carefully check any items that have been left outdoors before touching them. These critters go everywhere and the very moment you discover them by chance you and them usually are so close together that they start to fear for their lives and either flee or fight.

On each and every hike that we did on Tasmania, the two aforementioned Swiss women let me take the lead, asking me, only half in jest, to protect them from snakes. Most of our hikes took place in remote wilderness, trough primeval forests and shrub-covered highlands, along wide beaches of unsettled peninsulas and up mountains that gave panoramic views across forested,

Make a conscious effort to make it back home alive and healthy!

hilly areas devoid of any human life. These were days-long hikes and while they always followed man-made and well maintained hiking tracks, they still took us far from civilization. During those days we only briefly touched with the civilised world while we had to take to the road and pass settlements in order to shuttle from one hike to the next. One day, for the sake of change and for our own amusement, we once spontaneously did a quite different hike in the very midst of built up infrastructure: We had stopped for a break within a tiny village at a small roadside rest area. It was lined with permanently installed concrete tables set under a few trees. Right on the border of the rest area was the beginning of a very brief but broad hiking walkway. As is usual with Australian hiking trails, right next to its start stood a signpost explaining many details about it, the rules to abide by and the safety warnings recommended. Making us smile benignly was a piece of information that's never missing for a hiking trail: the total estimated walking time without breaks (which always isn't calculated as average of different walking speeds but with very slow hikers as point of reference). For this trail, the total estimated walking time was a total of five minutes only. From its outset, we could almost see it in its entirety: walls of green forest vegetation left, right – and at its end, which was partly visible from the onset, partly obscured behind a miniscule bend in the walkway. Compared to what we had accomplished, seen and experienced, this seemed like it would be a leisurely stroll down an unknown side street in the midst of an otherwise familiar city. For our amusement, we pretended to take this hike as serious as previous ones – donned our hiking boots and hats, threw a couple of supplies into our backpacks and strapped them firmly into place, set off wishing ourselves good luck and a safe return, then strode down the alley and – after what seemed like only a couple of steps – had to stop in front of the wall of green foliage at its end where we were beaming broadly about the "tough going" we just had successfully endured. We then turned around and headed back for the car park. But on the way back – the tables and the people resting there were already clearly into view, just a bit more than an arm's length away – the woman walking right behind me started to scream in fright and woe. I immediately turned around – my hart suddenly racing as if powered from an ongoing series of explosions insides of it – I found she was staring at the ground and thus I looked at exactly the same spot. But there was nothing there, so I continued to look around for the source of her agony – the cause from which she must be saved. By now my body was so pumped with adrenaline I was feeling more than ready to defend and fight for her. Only when several moments had passed like that did I discover a stumpy short snake winding quickly away from us trough the undergrowth next to the path, rushing to flee for its own safety. The woman who had discovered it was back in calmness much sooner than my blood came back to flow through my face.

The sole scorpion I ever saw in the whole of Australia was only a few centimeters short and almost invisibly transparent. It was after dusk just outside Jondaryan in the kitchen tent of the camping place on the compound of the big antique Jondaryan sheep shearing shed. The place was faintly lit up by a single naked light bulb hanging from the middle of the ceiling. It threw stark shadows, separating the kitchen into puddles of darkness and little kingdoms doused in glaring light, all of them sloshing in and out of each other every now and then when someone touched the tent involuntarily or a breeze came on, making the light bulb go on the swings of the power cord it hung from. When my eyes fell on the scorpion for the first time, at first all I saw were just a few black dots on the kitchen floor about three meters away from me. These dots had caught my attention because they had been moving across the floor and stayed in proximity to each other for quite a while now. At the edge of my perception, I had assumed them to simply be specs of dust being blown about by puffs of air, but for that they were moving at a speed to constant and in a line much too straight. So there I sat with bemused curiosity, now looking straight at those blotches in motion; eventually throwing a glance over my shoulder towards the light bulb to check: Were there any insects circling it that might've been throwing such shadows? There were none – and in any case they wouldn't have cast shadows moving in a straight line and at a constant, slow speed. It wasn't until the spots had approached me within less than a meter that I were able to make out the almost transparent scorpion's outlines. The small black shadows were his clearly visible inner organs. The scorpion walked with so much openness, lack of cover and self consciousness as if it took its surroundings as well as its presence in there for an absolute matter of course – as if it was fully complacent with itself and the world at large. However, the critter didn't went unnoticed. There were other campers present in the kitchen; standing next to me was a mother whose four children were playing a few meters further. She took note of the scorpion and, after half a second of consideration, decidedly set herself into motion towards it. She measuredly placed the heel of her shoe over it, then pushed down with all the force of her leg, twisting it a few times thoroughly with plenty of pressure – her face an open book filled with stories of determination, focused effort and heroism for the protection of the innocent (or so I later gathered). At that, I were perplexed as to why she had smashed a harmless looking critter? Asked about this, she explained to me (with a tone of pride in what she had just done and evidentness as if the reason for her behavior must of course be clear to all) the danger from which she had rescued us all (including especially her children for which she bore responsibility).

Tree-climbing ants

Ants in Australia are far bigger than any I've seen before. They bite sooner and harder. They're more poisoning and they've got better mutual coordination, always coming to help their friends and to fight alongside of them. They're accustomed to making their way towards their goals no matter what. They're quick walkers and they act decisively about how to deal with any obstacle which they might encounter.

I seated myself down under a eucalyptus tree in a shoreside park in Townsville. The tree had light grey and white bark that peeled off in thin stripes (a feature common with this species, evolved over time to pile up more tinder faster). The spot overlooked the lawn consisting of thick, dark-green (and surely quite drought resistant) leaves and beyond that the beach of fine grained sand on which waves broke that the strong incoming wind had crowned with foam, making the see appear like an approaching endless ball polonaise on the brink of raving all over town, with black blue gowns and matte white hair. Above all towered a granite sky that was so dark and frayed at its borders it was indistinguishable from the sea. I placed my backpack next to my knees, took out a book I had brought to read in the park and lent back against the tree trunk. I opened the book at once, started to read the first few sentences and felt something move on the skin of my chest (due to the warm weather, I wore no shirt). I assumed that an insect had landed on me that moment and waved my hand in its general direction to make it fly away while keeping my eyes glued on the book, continuing to read. But it didn't fly way whatever it was. Irritated, I put aside the book and looked down onto myself. There was a big, caramel and green colored ant sitting on my chest and it was about as large as the upper section of my thumb. For a long second I looked at it, half with bewilderment and half in admiration. Then I noted: It was not alone; there where five or six more ants, traversing my torso by its length – even though I had been sitting there since less than a minute ago. All of them were in motion, expect for the ant I had tried to wave off. I got up and – while rising – the tree trunk entered into my field of vision. For the first time, I spotted the road of ants careering up and down across it – and I noted an assortment of small blank-eaten animal bones at its foot. Always wanting to be kind to animals (as they can't consciously think and decide as well as us humans; thus I believe we should consider their interests when deciding about how to treat them), I considered briefly how to get the ants off of me without damaging them. I opted for flicking them off. So I cautiously tried to flick the first ant – the one standing still – off me with my finger. But it held on, shifting its pose slightly to absorb the sudden motion. It stood stiff and still for the next second – and then in one swift move it lowered its head to my skin and bit! It hurt! And then the other ants joined in – some came running towards the first, some stayed where they were, but they all did what the first had done! They all stopped doing whatever they had been doing and bit me! Alarmed, I turned to a couple sitting nearby on a picnic blanket and pledged for help to get the ants off me, and quick! They immediately grabbed their blanket from under them and brushed and knocked the ants off me (including the ones on my arms and legs which so far I had not noticed), until there were none left on my skin – I checked three times that they were all gone. I then stayed in my helper's presence for a while to have an insider ready to help in case I would've developed any symptoms.

While I were travelling in a friend's car in the area of Tom Price, a dove had crossed our path and gotten hit by the radiator grill while I was asleep in the co-drivers' seat. He later narrated to me how he had stopped the car and buried the bird. The following night, we stayed at a camping place – it wasn't one of the many fee-free ones that can be found all around Australia, but one that charged and in return offered – besides plenty of infrastructure and safety in numbers from throngs of other guests – supervisors. These came in handy soon: The next morning, after crawling out of our tents and upon approaching our car to prepare us breakfast, we discovered a couple of ants running around busily on the rear bumper. We wiped them away but immediately other ants entered the area. Unsuspecting, we opened the hatchback – that gave us view onto more ants running between our gear. Worried, we went on to open the rear side doors – even more ants! – then the front ones – even much more ants! – and finally the front lid. Ants everywhere – a milling mass like in the middle of an ant hill! The whole car was full of them! Apparently they had discovered the remains of the dead bird that we hadn't been able to clean away, then improvised a new road to transport them off. It lead lead up a rear tire and across the bumper, in through a brake light into the car, in between our luggage, under the rear bench that was folded down, towards the gear lever, through the lever box into the engine compartment and on the underside of the engine towards the radiator grill. Needless to say that our attempt at getting the ants away with a hand broom was ill-fated: Every sweep cleared only a little area that was immediately flooded again by other ants, making it

Make a conscious effort to make it back home alive and healthy!

look in less than a second as if nothing had been done at all. Clueless – even desperate – we turned to the campground's supervisors. They came over immediately with a spray can of insecticide (despite our protest against this drastic method), explaining that the ants were nesting close by, had been seen on the place before often and that this was the sole method that had turned out to be effective. Two brief puffs of this foamy concoction were enough to send all of the ants running for their lives. From one second to the next, they were nowhere to be seen anymore; their sudden fear for their lives seemed to linger in the air like a smell for slightly longer time. We checked the entire car and contents, yet all we could find were two pitiable, dead ants.

Crocodiles
You'll rarely come across warning signs against crocodiles, simply because Australians just don't venture to any places where crocs are or might be (this is: any place where there's water). If this doesn't make matters difficult enough for visitors from out of country, the following will: During the wet season, otherwise croc-free areas become croc-infested, striking water bodies as well as areas that are dry out of the season which become flooded (or flooded more). So, stay distant from water by several meters, even if on first, second and third look you can't spot any crocs anywhere near or far. Because Crocs submerge – waiting for prey in hiding is part of their hunting strategy and they usually stay out of sight as well as Nessie of Loch Ness does, so they cannot be spotted. Those images they show on TV of crocs in hiding may clearly show their eyes, budging at the waters' surface like little foam bubbles afloat, but in reality that is a rare sight. Crocs use that disguise rarely to only check every now and then; most of the time they're fully submerged and the waters usually are as

muddy brown as their skin. Further, those images on TV are immensely enlarged – otherwise they'd only show a brownish, contour-less water surface. Further: Even if you spotted two tiny foam bubbles floating several meters away on a pond or river, who would recognize that, let aside be alarmed by it? A calm, peaceful water body really is a deathtrap. And even if you're several meters away from the next croc: They react to even the tiniest movement of the water. Even from a large distance your movement from swimming, washing or brushing your teeth in a creek, or only from walking next to it, will draw towards you unwanted attention.

As I was told, crocs follow their nose rather than their eyes, since their eye sight isn't too well. And that they can out-run humans if running straight. And that they are slower to turn than humans, so that if they ran a curve or had to turn around, they would be much slower in comparison. The logical consequence of all that, as I was told, was that it would be possible to outrun a croc by running zigzag instead of straight. Other advice regarding how to deal with crocs which I were given without asking was that one could make a croc release its prey by hitting it hard on the nose or eye because these were the only parts of its body where they would feel pain. Now here's a reality check: Only very hungry crocs would get out of the water and run after prey. And would all this advice really work? Or are these stories based on hearsay and just ways to calm oneself down from agony – the fear of a real, sudden and unescapable lethal risk to ones' own life?

Dingoes
Dingoes are very big and wild dogs. As I were told, they would attack immediately when spotting prey. According to other reports, they're rather shy and prefer

to flee, unless they have food or children to defend. Additionally, they curiously gawk at everything new to them (such as humans turning up all of a sudden), appear out of the blue (because they're fast and run around much) and to them prey is everything which runs from them (as it triggers their impulse for hunting). A human can't escape from a Dingo: They can run about 40% faster than us (I'm here referring to Olympic athletes). Instead, during an encounter one should better not reveal any contact surface but rather stand tall, with arms folded and then slowly retreat with eyes fixed on the Dingo. Further, one should always supervise children in areas where dingoes are known to exist as those about waist-high animals (I'm here referring to my own waist – and I'm of very tall growth), are strong enough to be able to carry whatever is smaller than them (that includes toddlers already old enough to have mastered the crafts of walking and talking) and to even hurt grown-ups badly.

Sole time I met a Dingo so far was in a resort of camping huts on Fraser Island. Camp staff advised us of how to deal with Dingoes. With so many visitors to the island, those Dingoes that live there are accustomed to finding themselves close to humans. Staff mentioned that there was one showing up on the premises very frequently which could easily be identified by it having just three legs. The reason for its frequent visits was that it was hanging around in its home: It had been found wounded as a baby and was brought up hand-nurtured by camp staff. Because of that he was known to be friendly towards all humans. Now, hours later when we walked around the resort, all of a sudden a dingo turned up. He pranced around us happily. His tongue hung out of a corner of his mouth (giving him a facial expression of eagerness) and his eyes beamed like a pair of headlights looking out into nightly darkness. Immediately we froze in place and thought hard to remember the good advice we had been given about how to behave, while at the same time we were wondering whether we should defend ourselves or if this was that dingo familiar with humans – and in case it was, whether he could be dangerous even if he had been brought up by humans. However, before we arrived at any conclusion, the Dingo had jumped away on its three legs.

Leeches

Outfit yourself with suitably prepared clothes before venturing into areas where leeches reside. Wear long clothes and high reaching, enclosed shoes. On your shoes and legs, seal all openings and potential opening. Hungry leeches are very thin – and single-minded. They'd squeeze themselves through any opening no matter how tiny it may be – including holes for shoestrings or gaps between a shoes' top and tongue. Sticky tape comes in handy to seal gaps. Carry spare tape and whatever tools you need to apply it, to replace it immediately in case it falls off.

Magpies

Magpies are territorial birds which defend their domain against invaders during breeding season. Since they frequently reside in settled areas, this very frequently applies to persons going about their everyday activities. To deter invaders, magpies swoop them from behind (from the blind spot) towards the backs of their heads. While during most attacks this harmless-sounding behavior is all that occurs, they're nonetheless dangerous as a human fleeing from an attack might panic, stumble, fall off a vehicle the person's just riding or run into other (potentially lethal) dangers that are ever-present in road traffic when moving about inadvertently. Further, some

Make a conscious effort to make it back home alive and healthy!

magpies don't stop there, but additionally use their beak and claws with which they can cause severe injuries. So significant are the risks and damages that Australian environmental agencies inform about them extensively, including through TV-spots broadcast within breeding season ("Yes, it's that time of the year again!"). Some people have attempted to protect themselves trough disguises (such as wearing sunglasses on the back of their head or putting makeshift eyes made of round, black and white stickers onto their bike helmets) or to keep magpies at distance with passive measures (such as wearing pipe cleaners as spike imitation on bike helmets); but scientific studies revealed the whole lot of them to be useless – either magpies didn't notice them or they just switched to attack from the side, not the rear. What really helps to deter them (according to Australian authorities): Only trespass their territories in groups walking close together – wear broad rimmed hats or umbrellas (but don't deploy these to hit after magpies) – keep yourself at distance – keep your eyes fixed at them at all times. For bicyclists: decorate your bike with burgees – get off your bike and push it. And: never fight back. Magpies have very good visual memory and would only be more aggressive during their next attack (and since they remember people by their looks, they would then specifically target anybody looking alike the original attacker). Possibly that's why attentive observers found out that Magpies specialize: Some swoop only women. Some only swoop children. Some specialize by the color people wear. Some focus on cyclists. Some only defend against cyclists with black cycle helmets.

Authorities further recommend: If you encounter a magpie standing on the ground, brace your head and eyes and slowly retreat with your eyes fixed on the bird – because magpies that intend to hurl themselves from the ground upwards intend to hurt and destroy. These and other mischievous troublemakers should be reported to authorities. Other recommendations for the protection from magpie attacks: make detours, don't show up regularly at identical times and stay away from their territories entirely if you can – and: please feel encouraged to help your fellow people: If a territory that's being defended comes to your attention, put up homemade warning signs for them.

While I rode a bike around Gladstone, when briefly looking over my shoulder I noticed a black and white bird close behind me at about the height of my head. Certainly it was just passing so I looked ahead and didn't gave it a further thought. During the next several minutes, whenever I looked sideways or back, it was there, always flying about a meter behind me and firmly staying just out of my field of vision. I didn't knew I might have been at risk until I watched TV that night and for the first time saw the warnings.

Sugar cane toads

These big, moss-green toads look as calm and harmless as only toads can. But their poker face is just a blank facade because toads have no mimics. Cane toads are poisonous. In Australia, they have about no natural enemy and they know from personal experience they're at the top of the food chain. And in case anybody approaches them too closely, without dodging and without pulling even the tiniest bit of a face they'll spray everybody with generous doses of their poison.

Cane toads have been introduced to Australia (or better said, have been released deliberately at Australia's' north-eastern coast following pressure by sugar cane growers hoping for the toads to protect the cane from insets – too bad toads can't climb and those insect's habitat is in the upper reaches of the sugar cane). Every year they push the borders of their settlement area by about 40 kilometers. They go about just everywhere. Meanwhile they've spread all the way to Western Australia. There, individual toads with comparably longer legs have been found; the mechanisms of evolution have brought out this trait so there now are cane toads that can hike faster further. Cane toads have got nothing to fear (and they know of no threats because due to the size of the countryside the moment you meet them is the very first moment they've stepped straight out of their home: the wilderness). Thus, they can show up at any place at any time – and they'll never flee for cover but rather boldly stand out in full exposure. This includes hotel parking lots during busy uptime with a multitude of tourist groups rushing about. One evening after dark while I were having dinner at a hotel restaurant in Katherine, sugar cane toads emerged from the bush surrounding the parking lot, slowly hobbled forward and then just sat down placidly on the tarred surface that was dotted here and there with grass sprouting out of cracks and flood lit by the white light of street lanterns about as bright as the sun on a cloudy day. They then stayed firmly rooted in place. The floor-to-ceiling high glass windows gave us panoramic views onto that scene. Tourists leaving the restaurant went outside for the return walk towards their rooms. They discovered the toads and stopped immediately with excitement and fascination – just what tourists do when they're in a foreign country and encountering real-live specimen of a species that doesn't occur in their home country. They immediately stood themselves next to some of the toads, marveled at them, took pictures and alerted other tourists to their find, until a group had gathered, forming a circle of about ten people around one of the toads. That toad did: nothing. Expect (clearly visible from several meters away) breathing and spraying the onlookers' pants with poison several times (the flying drops of it glistened in the streetlamp lights like handfuls of diamonds casually thrown into a crowd) without the tourists taking note of what danger they were in. Luckily, hotel crew members did notice and collected the onlookers' pants. When they passed my table on the way to the hotel's own washing machine, I inquired whether it would be an idea to carry away the toads to keep visitors safe from them. In reply they shook their heads, explaining: Because of the immeasurable mass of toads, any resistance was futile. Thus, when travelling, beware of your excitement to encounter foreign wildlife. It will make you rush to marvel at it from up close – possibly too close.

Animals stealing food

Some animals have learned to help themselves to food claimed by us humans – more precisely: food in your ownership. However, they've not yet mastered to handle the obstacles standing in their way towards it by the methods we humans have thought out.

Park rangers service every national park, occupying themselves with duties such as maintaining the park and informing visitors about local sights, infrastructure and dangers. This is also true for Wilsons Promontory National Park. In that park, following a hiking path south for three days leads to a junction located in the middle of the forest. From there, an access path leads further south to scenic South Point, whereas turning left leads towards South East Point and then back to the park's entrance. Many hikers do both paths, first hiding most of their luggage at the junction, then doing a one-day trip to South Point and eventually returning to fetch their luggage and continue back via South East Point.

Leaving behind luggage is what local park rangers warn from, because ravens which live around the junction have discovered that luggage always contains food and that they can get to it by picking it open with their beaks. No, they won't act like humans do and bustle around with opening all the zippers, all the buckles and all the wrapping of your luggage and reseal them all when they're done filling their bellies with the food supplies you had provided for yourself.

At several camping kitchens on Tasmania and Great Keppel Island I came across locals who've already grown used to ignore the possums which had taken quarter under the roofs and from where they were keeping a close watch for to any upcoming opportunity and ventured out to help themselves to any food left standing around without asking or hesitation. To them, a brief moment in which you stray with your eyes away from your food is enough to catch what they want to grab from you and run away with and keep it, never never to hand it back.

I'm closing the section on dangerous animals with what I was once told, and what appeared to have happened on two of my own encounters: Most animals are only dangerous when defending themselves and would rather flee unhurt than stay, fight and thus risk their lives. Only a few species of animals exist whose members would hunt and attack humans on purpose, so learn which and where those animals are and simply stay away from those areas. When out in nature, walk loudly so that those animals who want to keep their distance can hear you from afar and run away before they start to feel trapped and forced to consider a fight against you as their only way out.

Now, people and animals aren't the only source of risk in the outdoors. There's one that's much bigger and is more mobile. And it's omnipresent.

Hazards – weather and environment

Climate in Australia is different from that on other continents. Give yourself at least a few days to get accustomed to it before setting out for any physical activity. Behaving as if the climate was similar to the one at the place you call home easily puts you at risk.

Sunshine
Australia lies under a hole in the ozone layer. Unfiltered UV rays hit onto the ground and anything on it (that includes: you). Unfiltered means: During winter (the season with lowest incoming radiation), the UV index in Australia is at and above three times that of Europe during summer (the season with highest incoming radiation).

I arrived in Sydney in winter. During my first day out and about, the sky was almost always entirely hidden behind steel-gray clouds. Very frequently rain showers passed and idled around on the streets as puddles long after having fallen down. Everything – buildings, trees people, cars, animals – looked similar like in a photograph with the color saturation toned down. Bales of dense fog (as sizeable as tall as well as wide people; floating at knee height above ground), very slowly made their ways between houses, parks or across pedestrian walkways, looking like little clouds that lost their bearings down from the sky and now were searching for someone they could ask for directions. Anytime the sun broke through the clouds, the difference which this made was significant: The bright sunlight gave everything clear contours, contrast and deeply saturated colors. Its warmth and energy immediately became sensible on the skin, as if one had gotten oneself covered all over in an armload of freshly prepared hot-water bottles, or filled the streets with radiant heaters working at their highest setting. Now, that was rare that day and I experienced it even rarer since I spent that first day in Sydney by visiting the sights. Since I already knew the exterior of the town's famous buildings from an early morning bus tour en route to my hotel, I now visited its museums and galleries – thus most of the day I stayed indoors in shaded rooms. I completed the ways between those places either on feet (walking in the shade of skyscrapers) or underground (on public transport) – and, as mentioned, the weather that day was densely clouded and foggy. But even then the sunlight was strong enough to cast shadows! By the end of the day, despite having seen very little sunlight, I found the UV radiation had been so strong that my skin had gotten tanned!

Heat

Most of Australia consists of arid or semi-arid desert. There (and elsewhere in Australia) temperatures to match can be found – the further up north the more. During some days, 40 degrees centigrade are easily exceeded – and it'll hit you out of the blue if you arrive unprepared.

The town of Yulara was founded at the end of the 1970s in order to concentrate and improve the infrastructure for tourists – as well as move it out of the national park, where it so far had grown uncontrolled. The flight there from Sydney took about four hours. It offered panoramic views over the beautiful, fascinating landscape: red desert, lined by blackened, dried out water courses and gray-white salt pans. We were shown movies because the flight took so long, but I rather kept my gaze on this exciting, foreign and fascinating sight. The airplane finally landed on plains covered in low green-gray shrub on red ground extending in every direction until the faraway horizons. Positioned just where the sky met with the horizon, there was standing the silhouette of Uluru – sandstone-red set against the sky which looked like the inside of a large blue enamel bowl turned upside down. From this distance, Uluru looked about as tiny as a fingernail. The plane rolled a bit on the pitch black asphalt until it came to a stop in front of the tiny white terminal building. Everything insides and outsides looked as what you'd expect upon arriving by airplane to a commercially serviced airfield, save for the uncommon looking surroundings beyond it. Upon peering out of the window, I noted a lot of usual activities: a marshaller directing our airplane entirely on foot, a tiny fueling vehicle pulling up, empty hand-pushed transport luggage carts brought closer. Likewise, events insides of the cabin appeared to me to just be business as usual: The signs advising to fasten seat belts got unlit, belt buckles clicked open all around, passengers rose and flight attendants opened a door for us to exit – at that very moment, the engines revved up and the aircon started to douse us passengers insides that cabin with cascades of chilly air. Sure, why not? After all, having an aircon run insides an airplane is just normal, isn't it? Normality continued, we passengers queued to exit, took out our luggage from the overhead lockers, picked up our newspapers and other personal belongings, shuffled slowly towards the exit door like a long parade in slippers, said our thank-yous and good-byes to the flight attendants and pilots who stood by the open door; finally I had awaited successfully to become the next one to get out: It was my turn to say good-bye.

Make a conscious effort to make it back home alive and healthy!

Just a step from the door I mentioned to the crew my gratitude for having gotten to fly Qantas again since (as each and every time) I had found it to be quite comfortable and enjoyable. I then turned towards the exit door, stepped through it and out and – that very moment, I immediately felt there was something noteworthy happening around me. Was it the surroundings? I took a quick look around, noted the wide open space under a huge clear blue sky overlooking the red plain with shrub cover until the horizon faraway – but that wasn't what my gut feeling was aiming to draw my conscious attention to. And then I felt it: All of my sweat glands – all over my body – were just springing into action, simultaneously and at full speed – like when a blue sky spontaneously decides to stage a heavy shower right there and then. It seemed to me like I had just passed through one of those typically narrow wooden doors with tiny inlaid glass window which lead into those lowly lit, wood-paneled rooms – I were out in a wide open space but the weather was so hot it was as if I had just entered a sauna.

When accustomed to the heat (or not knowing how hot it can get during a day), you may not realize the distress it puts you in. To explain that: The warning signs at the trail outsets for Uluru and for Kings Canyon have thermometers built in. The signs warn (in ten different languages, expertly translated): "Do not start this walk if the thermometer shows more than 30°C on or after 10am!" Because if it's that hot that early in the morning, temperatures are going to be even hotter at noon and thereafter – so hot that one dehydrates and dies of thirst faster than anticipated. Upon reading the signs I noted with curiosity the sheer number of languages. I mentioned that to a helpful-as-usual park ranger who stood nearby to one of them in order to answer visitor's questions. He pointed out that those warnings were targeted at those visitors who arrived via Yulara airport which was located close-by, because via it (and one of Australia's intercontinental airports) those places were accessible in less than a day from far away places where daytime temperatures were much more endurable and much less damaging and life threatening.

Natural disasters

Natural disasters can strike anywhere in Australia. Make sure to pick up the news and stay away from threatened areas – for your own protection and to not disturb ongoing rescue work.

The greater Darwin and Palmerstone area has been hit several times by tornadoes. Therefor storm shelters with meters-thick concrete walls have been built for residents. One of them is the Darwin Congress Center – like many modern office buildings it is made of much glass and steel; only that in this particular case it's a very little amount of glass and mountains of ferroconcrete. Signs at the building's corners indicate its function as storm shelter. Each sign is several square meters large and starkly contrasts the building – black script on orange background bolted on an inornate, plain gray-white building. Unerringly necessary as guidance for people trying to outpace a tornado coming close. All shelters in the area together can host 30.000 people. If that sounds like a lot more space than could ever be used: There's actually four times as many people living in the region. People are encouraged to prefer sheltering from storms in their homes – provided it's equipped with a storm proof room (as building laws require since being rewritten in 1974 following a devastating storm) Recommended alternatives to that are sheltering with friends or relatives in their home's shelter rooms or leaving the region entirely by heading south – perhaps as far south as Katherine, 300 kilometers away, in case that a storm would progress very far inland. On the same breath as that last advise, authorities recommend to inform friends, neighbors and relatives about one's departure, so that one won't be erroneously reported as missing. To those intending to sit out a storm within the region, authorities have a clear and tough message: At your own risk only – and prepare sufficient supplies of everything so that you can be fully self-sufficient for at least 72 hours until normal life recommences and infrastructure services are resumed.

Following a tornado hitting the east coast, my bank mailed me a letter, stating how they were rebuilding their flood-stricken infrastructure and outlets and listing temporary locations, opening times and additionally provided ATMs. Finally, they advised how I might regain access to my funds in case I had lost credit cards or other documents trough the storm. It was during that time that an ordinary man suddenly became famous and even attracted a fan club – he was live interpreter for sign language and always appeared next to Queensland's prime minister whenever he addressed the catastrophe-stricken public via TV as support for the deaf and hearing-impaired. People took a liking to him so much he even received fan mail with proposals of marriage.

Bush fires

Stay clear of areas where nature is on fire and act with caution where danger of fire exists – that includes about just everywhere since warnings from this danger are only given where it's extremely high and people are present to check on it. It's advisable to follow basic security measures no matter where: Do not lit open fires. If you do, remove everything that could catch fire beforehand within a radius of several meters. Extinguish a fire with earth or sand and (additionally) with water, then stand guard by it for a while to ensure it remains extinguished. Do not lit fires on days with low humidity or in very parched areas. Always have a bucket of water at hand. Don't park your car over burnable material as it might incinerate on a hot exhaust pipe.

For millennia and across many generations, Australia's' native inhabitants have burnt the meters high overgrown steppe in a controlled manner to attain better visibility of their prey and to prevent ignition of fires by flashes. Ideal preconditions for bush fires are still present today: hot, dry weather and dense vegetation which withers during the dry season. Making matters even worse is the fact that over time some plant species evolved so that they promote ideal preconditions for fires. Especially the species of eucalyptus trees has adapted to the selection pressure of frequent fires. Those trees are used to letting their seeds fall on ground that was freshly cleared by fires where they're almost without competition. Thus, bark peels off their trunks in long, thin and easily ignitable stripes. As if that wasn't enough, eucalyptus trees produce oil insides their leaves which helps fuel and spread fires. On a hot day, clouds of oil can be seen standing above eucalyptus trees which are looking similar to moving air above a heat source only much larger. Those clouds partially reflect the light and thus colorize it (that's where the Blue Mountains got their name from). You can even smell the oil from dozens of meters away. Eucalyptus trees are just waiting for a spark as fire starter. As I was told, a single spark is all it takes for a eucalyptus tree's oil cloud to explode into a great, raging and all-consuming ball of fire.

Snow and snowstorms

Australia has mountains more than 2000 meters tall. It snows heavily there during winter. Snowstorms from nearby Antarctica are bringing and throwing so many tons of icing onto the country that a significant portion of produce grown in Australia depends on irrigation fed by melt water courtesy of the most recent winter season. All that snow impacts the area's accessibility. That is why some remote settlements built specifically for employees of the hydro scheme intentionally don't sport any tourist facilities in order to deter visitors from staying so that long-hauled supplies for the permanent, needed residents will last longer whenever access roads are smothered with meter high snow again. It thus doesn't come as a surprise that some roads in the Australian alps are closed entirely during the months of snow season.

There are odd-looking walls standing on the mountains of Thredbo. They're several meters high and extend over quite some distance. They consist of metal poles every three meters webbed horizontally with a network of broad black rubber bands. What could be their purpose? Thredbo is a ski resort town and these walls are standing close to the ski runs – are they safety fences to catch skiers and snowboarders before they go over any ledges? Or are these awnings to catch the sunshine and provide shade from the harsh sun? Neither, but the term "catch" is the key: These walls were put into the flyway of storms which horizontally blow snow across the land (horizontally because the winds are so fast). Snow is caught when it hits against the fence's rubber bands, then falls down and piles up at the foot of the walls. The next morning, when the nightly storm has passed, piste maintainers push the masses with their snow groomers onto the ski runs, giving them a fresh cover – on a base layer of artificial snow, which was put there to cool down the ground because otherwise the ground would be so warm (heated by the sun's UV radiation which arrives to earth completely unfiltered due to the man-made hole in the ozone layer) that any snow would melt immediately after falling. But this artificial snowmaking can only commence if nighttime air temperatures are low enough for water drops, hauled by snow cannon into the air, will freeze into snow crystals. In order to nonetheless enable hoteliers to plan with confidence, they've mutually agreed to let the winter season begin on the very same day every year, no matter how much (or if at all!) snow lies on the slopes. Thus, Australian ski season officially starts on Queens' Birthday, and from that day onwards hotel and lift operators will bill you full price (without turning red with shame) for ski passes which you've booked ahead and for hotel rooms (which cost double as much during season as off season) even if the scenery outsides looks rather summery and you cannot undertake a single ride.

Flash floods – and flash floods in (parched) river beds and canyons

When it rains it pours in Australia. There's an ocean's supply of water all around the continent and a hot climate which continuously evaporates loads of it. Clouds then foray inland in long convoys and no mountains which could stop them stand in their ways. The ground below, baked and hardened from the sun, isn't ready to soak up sudden downpours of water which thus flows off overground as flash floods, frequently going a long way for hundreds of kilometers. You'll frequently come across almost or entirely parched river beds or canyons. Refrain from venturing into them because a flash flood might be on its way to hit you out of the blue.

In Cairns and Darwin I saw gullies with bars so far apart you could easily stick a foot trough them. I used to believe they were damaged; anytime I passed one of them I wondered why no-one made to fix them but rather they were left in such dangerous disrepair – until one night when my mother and me wanted to have dinner, but in the hotel where we stayed nothing was being provided. It was during wet season – off-season – and there were hardly any guests residing there. The hotel restaurant was closed, supposedly because of too little business. The adjacent bar was open, but they didn't serve food. All the barman could offer us were bar snacks and a recommendation: There was a restaurant further up the road out front and leading along the beach. It would still be open for the next fifteen minutes. He gave us precise directions, then returned to taking care of the other patrons present: a couple sitting on the large terrace under palm trees by the pool – in the ensemble they looked like a drop of ink in a large jug of water. So, we walked across the hotel grounds (pools under eucalyptus trees, in the blackness of the night lit up by orange and turquoise spotlights) then turned onto the street; bare asphalt with no sidewalk but gullies every few meters; to our right beach with surf lightened by the orange-red light of the street lamps; on our left first another hotel and then solely a string of bungalows on stilts. On our way, it started to rain. First it was just a drizzle, but then full-on monsoon rain set in. It was pouring down like a waterfall – all around us and as far as the eye could see – lit up by light from the houses, by the glow of the city center further down on the bay and by a street lamp every dozen meters.. The image of heaven opening all gates was the reality through which we were moving – feeling – breathing – during those minutes. We continued onwards, because the restaurant was about to close soon, we were in the midst of it all anyway and that evening and in this remote part of town it was our only hope of getting food. Within moments, the clear, warm rainwater rose about knee high. Luckily we had aptly dressed for the high temperatures (shorts and sandals) and had precautionary packed rain ponchos made of plastic foil so that our clothes didn't get too soaked. We passed a few of those manhole covers that before I had believed to be damaged. Now it showed they had been designed so with a purpose in mind: Try to keep the floods in check and get as much of them off the road as fast as possible.

Lake Eyre in Southern Australia can be found on most maps, even though it rarely ever contains any water at all. Its tributaries evaporate in the desert heat or get lost flooding back and forth on the very flat plains. It only happens once every couple of years that flash floods from strong monsoon rainfalls fill it. These floods gather from as far as Queensland and the Northern Territory (several hundred kilometers away). Plant and animal species have grown accustomed to springing to life on the spur of the moment and so have the local sailing club's members: When the lake gets filled, Australians travel in and flock there like laypeople to the stock markets whenever there's an investment bubble on the brink of bursting. The amount of water is huge always – light aircraft owners go on scenic flights to overlook the large surface. The largest amount of water that ever arrived within one year was 34 cubic kilometers. Since Lake Eyre lacks an exit, water departs it by evaporating, which takes months due to the size of the floods. The water first becomes so briny that specialized algae bloom and colorize it. Finally the time between floods recommences and Lake Eyre again is a salt flat extending from one horizon to the next. Notice how big Lake Eyre is when you look at a map. That's how much water pours down and traverses the country in a matter of just a few weeks, passing through parched beds, floodplains and canyons on the way.

Make a conscious effort to make it back home alive and healthy!

So, read warning signs (if present) and apply your common sense (especially where there are no signs). Some signs are in-your-face – but sometimes there are none because some dangers only become apparent when they reveal themselves by striking for the first time, so that warning signs about them can only be allotted once it's to late for those affected by their first occurrence: In Queensland there's a spot where a rural road passes by a national park. A small rest area has been built there with four permanently installed wooden tables. Immediately adjacent lies a river bed which is filled with boulders so abraded they're round; they're sized small and large up to three meters in diameter. Large warning signs stand next to the river bed. Prior to them at the entry of the rest area, a commemorative plaque fashioned from dark green marble has been installed. It tells about a young man who stopped there while travelling through with his family. He climbed around the boulders, became stuck between them and then was surprised by a flash flood. The plaque says "He came for a break – and stayed forever." It's a very short path between river bed and entry to the rest area, but on those few meters there are a total of five warning signs that explain the risk in detail.

A saying recommends: "When in Rome, do like the Romans" because it's a good idea to learn from the people whose ancestors – generations of them – collected experience on how to stay alive and well and then ensured to pass them on in the form of recommendations. Aborigines do just that since millennia. And they share some of this knowledge with all people: In the Karijini National Park visitor center, an exhibition speaks about the area's history prior to settler's arrival. As part of it, locally residing indigenous communities ask visitors (that's you!) to not venture into the canyons – the entire region is strewn with deep, narrow canyons. Simply being in there is dangerous to life, because it frequently happens that clouds dump their load in one place of this area and that these floods flow onwards through the canyons. On the way they've got to squeeze through between canyon walls (which stand very close together everywhere) and the pressure from that accelerates the floods and turns them into lethal flash floods that hit out of the blue (and up to several hours later) in places dozens of kilometers away where it didn't rain but instead only a few clouds were visible faraway on (or even beyond!) the horizon. It even happened that rescue helpers came to the aid of hikers that had fallen and suffered broken bones (evacuation from the canyons usually only possible by helicopter because of the steep, narrow and twisting canyons) and during preparation of the injured for transport were surprised by floods.

Soft beaches
Even if the ground looks solid enough to walk or drive across it, actually it might not be.

Mackay has a very broad and scenic beach, dotted with tiny areas that are covered in a bit of water. I discovered it while touring the town on a bike and from the beach side road I spotted in the distance people enjoying a walk by the shore where the waves were breaking – under an Yves Klein-esque blue sky appareled with white clouds like a series of quick brushstrokes thrown on a canvas. The whole picture almost looked like a painting. Spontaneously I decided to join those people, become part of the art and (since I was on a bike) cycle along the shore. To save myself the detour to where the shore met the road (the shore was leading in a wide curve to a point several dozen meters away from where I was standing) I set to drive across the beach in a perfectly straight line towards where the people were (I didn't took notice of the fact that they were keeping close to shore). So I put myself in motion, got off the road and on the beach, and set off straight ahead. On my way I covered only about two meters, then the bike sank in up to half of the wheels into soft, soaked sand. I didn't let that change my plan. I got off the bike, pulled it back out, retracted to the road, chained the bike to a lamppost, immediately turned around and set off to walk the distance on foot. On my way I sank into the sand again and again – so much that it almost pulled the shoes off of me. I didn't let that change my plan. When finally pulling out my shod foot took me a lot of troublesome pulling I finally took my shoes and socks off, stuffed them into my backpack and rolled up my pant's legs. Then I continued onwards. It got worse a few meters on. I started to sink in up to my knee, so I took off my pants and continued onwards just sporting the swimming trunks which I was wearing beneath my clothes. I didn't let that change my plan. Lucky for me I had come so aptly prepared, because this sinking into the sand and pulling myself out continued all the way to the water's edge, alternating between getting to walk on solid, bright sand (feeling dry and sun-warmed under my feet), and just steps further (sometimes the immediately next step), sudden sinking into chilly wetness without prior warning – sometimes up to the top of my hip. When finally I reached the shore (a strip of solid sand about six meters wide lying next to the surf) I didn't mingle there for long with the other people ambling there as I had planned initially, but sat down exhausted and rested for a moment. Then I made my way back out to solid land. On that return walk, I carefully traced the other promenader's steps which they had left behind in the sand, to ensure I got to walk on the solid, albeit (for a good reason) more trodden path. I had changed my plan and didn't return on a straight similar to the one on which I had arrived – because, sometimes, a straight way isn't the shortest; sometimes detours lead to a goal faster and easier.

Sea currents

The sea around Australia has heavy currents and (due to the closeness to the equator) high tides. The upside of this is that it makes for great surf. The downside is that it can catch swimmers and drag them out – or worse, submerge them (some pedestrians in shallow beach break have gotten pulled by waves out to sea). Therefore, many towns along the coast have a Surf Life Savings Club – these are etched into Australia's culture and their volunteer members train with sportsperson's ambitions to go and aid people in the surf by running and swimming (or rowing in boats) towards and rescuing them. They serve shifts to watch over parts of the beaches, securing only the flag-marked areas, hence the recommendation: "Swim between the flags" which usually is followed by: and only if signals are up that it's safe to swim, that lifeguards are on duty and that the weather is calm enough to enter the sea and come back out alive.

Lifesaving in aquatic environments by swimming and rowing boats are officially organized sports. Competitions are staged all over the globe, as well as biannual world championships. In Australia, Surf Life Savings Clubs compete in regional and national leagues. Further, they take care of educating the public, teaching people safe behavior at the beach and in the surf and sea. There even exists a club in Kalgoorlie Boulder (340 kilometers inland from the nearest shore) so that anyone venturing to the ocean will be aptly warned and prepared.

Make a conscious effort to make it back home alive and healthy!

This ends the chapter on hazards ever-present around you from surroundings and environment. There are more that you encounter when you're passing through that – an amalgamation of all sources of hazards I've described so far: Weather and climate, you yourself, other people as well as organizations. Outdoors is where one comes across each other.

2. DANGERS WHEN GETTING AROUND

If you opt to not stay in one location, the seemingly simple activity of getting around will expose you to risks from doing just that.

Getting around – on the road

It takes very little effort to opt for a travel mode where someone else takes care of all the driving and organizing efforts. But organized group tours are costly and someone else (not you) sets itinerary and duration of stopovers. Australian train connections (if existing at all) are comparatively slow. Australian overland bus lines only run a few times daily (or less frequent) and solely take you from one settlement to the next without stopping at all the interesting sights in between. But despite all these drawbacks, these modes of travel have one huge advantage: Those sitting behind the steering wheel and those responsible for organizing know about road risks peculiar to Australia.

crossing the road
Since driving is on left in Australia, before crossing the road you should first look right. To help you get accustomed, most inner-city road crossings in Sydney bear large arrows and "Look right" lettering painted on the ground at their outset.

During the 1996 Olympic Games in Atlanta (USA), a journalist got hit by a car. This visitor from Australia had looked in the wrong direction (and not both ways either) before commencing to cross the road.

During the 2000 Olympic Games in Sydney, a journalist got hit by a car. This visitor from the USA had looked in the wrong direction (and not both ways either) before commencing to cross the road.

Left side driving

Even if you haven't spent much time conducting a motor vehicle: If you grew up in a country where driving is on right, it'd be so ingrained that it would be easy to forget that all driving is on left in Australia.

The Bavarian woman and the Scotsman with whom I once got to travel with owned a dark brown station wagon. They called it "Ducky", even though it didn't look anything alike a duck. According to their casually explanation, that name was derived from a piece of silver duct tape which was affixed left from the steering wheel, and said piece of tape was all that remained from the previous owner's "reminder to self" notice. I forgot about it right thereafter, but it came back to play a part following a break which we took at a tiny resting place next to a rural road (a concrete table set under two trees – the only ones near and far). There, the two told me they were usually taking turns at driving during road trips and since I was now part of the travel party on this journey, a homey of their in-car crowd, they asked me sit in the driver's seat and take the wheel for a while. Thus came my first time in Australia that I took a car to the road – after already having spent several months in that country. I performed the usual routine: closed the door after getting in, adjusted seat and mirrors, buckled up, checked that everyone else insides the car had buckled up (my two travel companions had sat down on the rear bench seat), started the engine, steered the car onto the street at slow pace and – in the very moment that I was going to push down the gas pedal to accelerate, the two kindly jumped at me (as if they had just been waiting for it), remarking that there was a very good and real reason why the piece of duct tape had been affixed left from the steering wheel and not opposite or in any other place: Out of habit and without thinking I had steered the car into the wrong lane. Luckily that had lasted for only a few meters and (as very common in Australia outsides of towns) there was no other traffic.

New South Wales is popular – it's home to most Australians. Splendidly constructed roads connect the many towns, yet traffic is so little that two lanes per road are enough and almost always are all there is. New South Wales is popular with tourists and immigrants, too. To advise them, signs are standing guard next to major country roads, reminding drivers with both arrow icons and text: "Drive on left in Australia!"

It really takes constant reminders to retrain, as it does to resettle after returning home: Upon arriving in Germany a friend of mine got picked up at the airport by her parents. They greeted each other, picked up her luggage, went to the parking lot, put the luggage into the boot and then she ambled along the car's side towards its front in order to get into the passenger seat. When she stopped by the door, she noticed with surprise that her father was standing right behind her. With an amazed look on his face he held out the car keys to her, asking with disbelief in his voice: "Do you want to drive?"

It was a tad different when my parents picked me up. They, too, met me at the airport in Frankfurt / Main. We took the autobahn that runs past it; the two were sitting in the front with my father behind the wheel. For two hours we drove on it and talked, then close to my hometown we left by an exit. Shortly behind that we came to a roundabout. The the other roads which opened out into it were poorly visible due to a small hill in its center and trees besides the roads. Nonetheless, my father swiftly drove into the roundabout and – much to my shock and surprise! – took a shortcut trough it – sudden, rapid and very risky! My jaw dropped instantly into bottomless nothingness. Shocked, I immediately inquired why he had done so. I wondered to myself: Had he determined so quickly that the roundabout was free from other cars – despite poor visibility? At that moment we already had exited the roundabout and were driving onwards on another road. I twisted in my seat to look back at the roundabout – over my shoulder and through the rear window – in order to persuade myself that we really hadn't been in any danger at all from any oncoming traffic. That second, my father answered my question with a simple "Beg your pardon?" Apparently, or so it seemed, he hadn't heard me properly, so I repeated louder: "Why did you take a shortcut?". That instant I noted that all signs at the roundabout were indicating the wrong direction! Confused I continued "...and why are all the signs indicating the wrong direction?" Following this, silence hung insides the car for a second, then my father grasped what I erroneously believed and laughed surprised. It took me a few moments to understood what had made him. It took me eight full months, much persuasion and a test in a controlled environment (single-direction autobahn with separate lanes) until he would lend me his car again. Conclusion: The correct side to drive on isn't a law of nature but just habit and social convention.

Drunk drivers (also known as bloody idiots)
Do not drive during twilight or at night. Roads and most road hazards on or next to them are unlit and thus only

poorly visible or even totally invisible at night. Among the risks on the road which one can meet head-on at night are: other drivers – especially those ones who've consumed alcoholic beverages yet even so believe themselves to be in a state where they can drive themselves home and arrive there undamaged after a night out drinking – even though by now everybody should know: "If you drink, then drive, you're a bloody idiot!" (Quoting from the world-famous public education campaigns of the Transport Accident Commission (better known by its abbreviation TAC), the statutory insurer from which all vehicle owners in Victoria must take out liability insurance.)

The cheapest hotel rooms in outback Australia are pub stays: rooms on the floors above from a bar, initially put there to host patrons who got themselves too drunk to drive themselves home safely.

Unfortunately there are people who get behind the wheel drunk intentionally. I once got to speak to someone who does. He was working as farm hand on a sheep station where I stayed as a guest. He was the eldest of six children of the family next door which operated a farm, too. According to his twisted logic his actions were all right since on his way home (after getting drunk) he'd only drive on remote and barely frequented roads where it was hardly likely anybody but him was on the move; thus if he had an accident (so he told himself) it would only affect him and him alone. On top of that he was sure he wasn't clashing with the law since police was usually remote from there (as if written and enforced law was the only one existing and there weren't a moral duty to pave the way for us human's good coexistence). Too bad that despite his assumptions chances are highly likely that on the road at night he'd hit upon someone or something. Too bad he didn't consider the feelings of his (or your) family in case of any accident and that he as the oldest of his siblings was being a bad role model to them. Too bad that police likes to crack down against misdemeanor with broad, coordinated checks. Too bad he was constantly hurting himself and turning a blind eye towards that. Because of his constant drinking, he was always out of money and according to his twisted logic it was okay to sell the car his parents had presented him with as he needed one for his commute to work on the neighbor's farm (which they had arranged for him as preparation to take over the family farm). Now, is this person an isolated case that can be easily avoided? Not at all: TAC's campaigns have been continued since many years ago. Meanwhile, they comprise countless advertising spots and information made available in other media. They lead to some success: Every year there are less people dying from road accidents compared to previous years. But every single person that had to go is – gone. TAC's longest spot so far is a documentary. It portrays friends and family members of a person who erroneously had assumed himself to be able to steer a car despite being drunk. The documentary shows how they try to cope and how they still suffer – a whole year later.

Floods

Since both floods and flash floods only occur once in a while, for many roads no bridges or causeways have been constructed across the wide and (most of the time) parched water courses and flood plains. Instead, there are other aids.

If you find water on a road: Check if it's shallow enough for your car to make it to the other side before you start attempting to pass through it.

How to survive travelling in Australia

It was a regular day on a guided bus tour through the Northern Territory. We were on the road from one town to the next and the bus windows gave view onto green grassland left and right. Thin white sticks stood along the country road in regular intervals every dozen or so meters. Suddenly, the loudspeakers jumped to life with the tour guide's voice – with his Swiss accent, he explained to us the white stick's purpose: "This is for the case that there's water on the road, because that is dangerous!" To that, the tourist sitting which sat next to me on the other side of the alley turned a baffled and then a puzzled face – you could almost see the cogs turning behind his forehead. Then all of a sudden his face cleared like the sun breaking through rain clouds, he slapped his forehead in sudden understanding and exclaimed with delight "Ah! Aquaplaning!" Not sharing his excitement, one of us travellers sitting around him then politely pointed out how the sticks that still paraded past our bus in motion were reaching up higher than aquaplaning ever could – even higher than the bus itself (despite the fact that Australian tour buses are extraordinarily tall). That's how heavily flooded Australian roads can get.

While travelling the Northern Territory, upon driving across bridges it happened very frequently that I looked out of the car window and down and noted that there was another bridge between those ones which I were driving on and the river bed far down below. Those lower bridges always looked perfectly fine and ready for use, yet always at each of their ends they had no connections to any roads. Apparently, they had been abandoned in exchange for higher ones constructed immediately above them. Even though the river beds below carried only very little to no water, overall bridge level had apparently nonetheless been raised to allow uninterrupted flows of people, wares and traffic while floods passed through. Because one can only pass through water with vehicles which are aptly equipped and adapted for this purpose.

If you come across a flooded stretch of road, don't think your car could make it through simply because you witnessed somebody else achieve that. An eyewitness told me how she had to watch someone commit such folly. It was on the road between Yulara and Alice Springs; floods had stopped the tour bus she was on, other vehicles were queuing up. While the passengers waited for the situation to change, standing around next to the bus, some tourist drove his rental car into the water. Prior to that, he'd spoken with the people waiting and many of them had tried to keep him from performing this foolery, but he was stubbornly persuaded of his plans because a bit of time ago he had seen how a car had crossed the water successfully. He was blind to the fact that his car was an ordinary limousine, while the car he had seen cross the water was an aptly prepared 4WD – perhaps he wanted to ignore the facts, since he felt breathing down his neck were both an agreed return date for the car at a rental station in Darwin and already booked return flights back to his home country He was so fixed on making it that it didn't cross his mind that such dates can easily be rescheduled upon request and at very little to no cost (and as I were told later, some rental car companies in Australia are very accommodating to customers if returns aren't made on time due to blocked road). So, this driver steered his car into the water. It immediately entered into the car's air intake – deployed for engines to receive fresh air for the combustion process. This drowned the engine instantly so that it stopped working immediately – while the car was still in the water, where it thus came to a full and complete stop. The water continued flooding in, now starting to seep into the passengers' cabin (which usually aren't water-tightly sealed). To flee the dangerous situation, the passengers wanted to get out but due to the water outsides pushing against the doors, these couldn't be opened. Thus all passengers had to wiggle their way out through the windows. They were still wading back to dry land when another aptly prepared 4WD passed from their car and them from the other direction. Together with the waves it caused, the current of the floods pushed their limousine off the (slightly elevated) road and into deeper water right next to it, where it sank completely. As said eyewitness travelled on shortly thereafter, I don't know how the story ended (Recovery! Draining! Missed flights!), but damages arising from natural catastrophes and from deliberate acts of the renter are fully at renter's cost, according to T&C of rental companies.

Rental car insurance coverage

Strict regulation applies to car insurances, too. So check the conditions and make sure to follow them – or take out one that covers all that you require.

Sometimes insurance coverage is only valid when the car is on tarmac at all times. Yet it's easy to find unpaved roads. Even major roads have stretches solely made of gravel, in part or in full. Most roads in national parks and in camp grounds are bare or corrugated earth, and farms out back sport ways made of soil which road construction authorities grade about once a year. While travelling western Tasmania, I didn't see tarmaced streets for days.

4WD (four wheel drive) and no experience

Before setting out in a 4WD car, make sure you know how to drive it properly (especially off of paved roads, which most likely is what you're renting that 4WD for).

Make a conscious effort to make it back home alive and healthy!

That means: take sufficient driving lessons and train yourself.

Australian Automobile Assistance found that most of the cases where they're called to help with a 4WD are simple to solve – at least for the assistants coming to aid. They almost always encounter drivers unable to cope with 4WDs which got stuck in a wrong combination of levers where a simple changes of these are all it takes to get them 4WDs going again. But don't ask me how to accomplish that – I only know driving 4WDs from being taken for a ride. If you are stuck: Did you already try other combinations of lever settings or check for advice in the manual? Good luck and happy searching!

Getting stranded: Stay with the car!

In case your car can't move onwards while you're on an overland drive between cities and/or roadhouses, stay with the car no matter if it got bogged, broke down had an accident. Reason being: You'll be found sooner; cars can be spotted much easier than humans, from the ground as well as from the air out of rescue team's light aircraft. From a distance, cars are brightly colored rectangles which stand out vividly from their surrounding (guess why in 2004 the livery of Greyhound Australia's overland coaches was changed to fire engine red from the classy McCafferty's celebratory gold which looked a lot like camouflage against bare, bronze-brown soil). But people appear from a distance like small black dots. And out there, the open plains are covered with vast quantities of black dots. Plus, a car is very useful in the outback, even if it doesn't run any more. The features it provides include: It shelters you from wild animals, shades you from the heat of the day and from the burning sun radiation – and it's a storage room for all the drinking water you hopefully brought because need to replenish during the day what you sweat out due to the heat. The supplies in your car save you from dehydration.

You've spot someone who got stranded: Keep driving on!
In case you see a stranded car along the road, keep driving without stopping! It might be a trap! Instead, keep moving on and leave providing assistance to the police. You can alarm them from your mobile phone or at the nearest settlement or rest stop. Even with the delay this will cause, help will arrive soon enough despite the country appearing to be a large void. For this reason and purpose, Australian authorities are equipped with fast cars.

When driving with friends from Katherine to Broome, we repeatedly passed stranded cars – most of them occupied by aboriginal families. Each time which we passed such a site, sticking to aforementioned advice (which we had received as a warning from police people), we felt perplexed as to what might have happened to them – and if they possibly might actually be in need of immediate help. Once – just once – we decided to stop and risk it despite the warning and check for ourselves. For our own protection, we passed the place and halted our car about a dozen meters away, so that those who were to remain seated in the car could take flight in case of a threat. I alone got out of the car and walked towards the people which stood next to the stranded car. On the way I talked courage into myself and intentionally ignored that legs had turned to jelly – and then I addressed those waiting, inquired about their situation and against expectations didn't find neither a threat nor an emergency situation, but solely frustrated people with no plan but a car with an empty tank, asking me not for petrol but for a cigarette to calm their nerves. My next question reveled that they hadn't brought drinking water. I walked back to the car and we decided to act both resourceful and reasonable and spare for them a few liters of bottled water from the supplies we carried with us. Upon handing that over, I promised them to alert somebody in the next town to come and help them. And so we did; as soon as we arrived there, we immediately drove to the local police office, entered and reported our sighting to an officer. His comment to that was a sighed "Oh no, not again!" and "It keeps happening to them, they are too careless!" (to which I'd comment that maybe they had just miscalculated their fuel supply). Immediately he grabbed his uniform jacket and walked out the door in order to leave and go to their aid. We walked out almost directly behind him. He was quick – just when we were crossing the threshold, he was already pulling out of he parking lot in a police car – and I couldn't help but notice its peculiarities: It had an outfit which is typical for police cars assigned to law enforcement officials in the outback: ten cylinders, 30 centimeter wide slick tires and a three meters tall radio antenna as thick as an arm, erected on a bumper reinforced so much it was double the original size.

Rail crossings

Almost all rail crossings are unfenced and the signage which warns from them usually stands less than a meter prior to them. Further, these signs are very unobtrusive: no flashy colors – just a cross painted white, sometimes supplemented with a really tiny light that flashes in red while a train is approaching. Making matters worse is that quite a few rail crossings lie hidden behind road bends or trees. If you encounter a rail crossing while you're on the road, it's usually sudden and surprising.

Intersections between rail and road are a fairly new thing in most of Northern Australia. The sole railway connection (the single-track Darwin – Alice line) was completed and opened just a few years ago. Back then, all government outlets I saw showed posters advising citizens about the danger, the new signs and their meaning. But did all the locals got the message comprehended how to behave safely around rail tracks in order to save themselves from the danger? The day following the inaugural train journey along the Alice – Darwin line, I read an interview with its conductor in a paper. He reported that during said journey he constantly had been energized (despite the line not being electrified) because he had to pay much more attention than on a usual train journey. The reason being: A train line through the entire Australian continent from North to South had been at the planning stage for more than a hundred and forty years. There had been several attempts prior to that, all of which were halted long before construction was anywhere near complete. That was reason enough for thousands of people to come and celebrate when at last the line was opened, welcoming the first train passing through with bonfires. All revelers cheered on the train as it came and passed – many positioning themselves immediately in the road tracks in front of the oncoming train, stepping asides only at the very last moment, causing the conductor to drive so slowly that the inaugural journey arrived several hours past schedule.

Road trains

Road trains aren't the same as lorries. They're significantly longer and have no mud guards and aren't at all identical to each other but come in various lengths and diverse combinations of engines and trailers. On public roads one usually only encounters only the small and the tiny variants, consisting at most of one engine, three trailers and far too many giant wheels to count; walls of wheels which look like the tire pile safety walls that stand besides race tracks – only horizontal and turning fast: that's a road train in motion, seen up close at eye level.

Because of their length, turning, swerving and dodging takes road trains plenty of time as well as much more room than is available anywhere on the open road. Thus they simply never swerve, never dodge. If you see one coming at you, dodge out of their way and stay there firmly until it's past you. The person at it's steering wheel expects from you to get yourself into safety. And what in case that you don't, might they...? No, they'll never break and get their vehicle to a standstill in time because they simply can't: Road trains are incredibly heavy and therefor have a very long braking distance. According to my own observation, even the tiniest ones with only one engine and one trailer need at least more than a hundred meters of full braking until they've come to a standstill.

Road trains are too long to be overtaken (unless you can oversee the road ahead until the horizon and it's completely void of oncoming traffic), but it will happen frequently that they overtake you. This will be a common occurrence if you stick to the speed limit as truck drivers frequently don't.

Road train drivers are aware that their vehicles can kill and that should an accident occur they'll be the ones walking (or driving) away from the scene alive, unhurt and healthy. Sadly, in many cases that hasn't lead to aptly adapted behavior patterns and driving styles, but to attitudes contemptuous of life.

Worse, on top of all that due to the long distances in Australia and the sparseness of places where drivers might get exchanged, it happens too often that drivers overstep the driving period permitted by law (and recommended based on scientific evidence) and risk falling asleep at the wheels of their super-heavyweight vehicles while these push on headless at high speed, bulldozing through anything that might stand in their way.

Following an hours-long drive across open land, we reached the outskirts of Geraldton. Prior to that, we had the road almost completely to ourselves, but suddenly we arrived at a road intersection that was crowded with moving cars. And through that mass of cars in front (and around) us was cutting a road train engine painted in shiny metallic black. It was three times taller than the cars, towering over them like a castle-topped mountain over a valley filled with humble huts. The bright sunlight was both absorbed by it as well as reflected by its shiny chrome parts. And on the top of its grill sat a visor. (Road trains and many other vehicles are equipped with visors and other protective gear to deflect damages during collisions. A visor is a usually clear strip of plastic which is installed horizontally and transversely to the direction of travel at the top and front above the grill. Further there are roo bars made from solid metal ("roo" is Australian for Kangaroo). Some vehicles are equipped with grilles which fully cover their windows in order to prevent objects from smashing them in and advance into their interior.) Some people label their visor, similar to others who affix bumper stickers to their cars. Now, while that black engine was cutting through the traffic like a tuna hunting through a school of fish, we too were driving onwards with the wave of traffic. It swept us directly in front of and past the black engine. When we passed it, for a moment all that could be seen from the windows on one side of our car was: its grill. I sat immediately next to one of those windows, and visible high above me (right next to the last small strip of blue sky) was the black engines' black visor, with writing in white letters that said "Hasta la vista!" – a last message to those seeing and experiencing how this engine came at them up close. I believe that this message sums up quite well what road train drivers think and feel for humans and other living beings which don't pull over (or jump on) in time to escape from them into safety.

As mentioned, road trains are uncommonly long. Is it the same with their width? Quite to the contrary: They're at most 2.5 meters wide as prescribed by law – they thus can fit into a single regular lane. Only once in the whole of Australia did I encounter a vehicle on an open road which exceeded the official maximum size. It was the Thredbo ski bus which shuttled back and forth between both ends of the resort town past valley stations and hotels. It had been extended by attachment of a rack for skis, poles and snowboards onto its exterior. While the bus had been painted black and covered with advertisement, almost nothing of that was visible, because even though the annex made the bus just a few centimeters wider than permitted dimensions, it had to carry appropriate warning signs. These were so huge they largely concealed the bus. In black on neon orange they almost shouted "OVERSIZED" from afar – such warnings really are regarded as necessary because oversized vehicles are so uncommon in Australia, different from road trains which every Australian knows about, inclusive of the risks which those carry with them.

Among of the sources of risk can be the person at the wheel and how they deal with their level of fitness. It was in a roadhouse in Western Australia that I came across something which made me really worried about the way they do that. Said roadhouse lies (as is frequent in Australia) a few hundred kilometers from the nearest stop in both directions of the road – which (as is frequent as well) are roadhouses, too. We arrived there late in the evening; it was beaming as bright as a permanent flash light in the surrounding nightly blackness that had befallen the world around it. There, in the mini-supermarket adjacent to the filling station, a shelf overflowing with Thermo Cups caught my eye. They bore the roadhouse's logo and were bright pink with yellow lids. Adjacent to them hung a sign promising each buyer of said cups a free refill during every visit to this roadhouse. Now, while in general that might've been to support several Australian roadhouse's efforts to reduce accidents from diver fatigue - they've opted into a program of providing free coffee to encourage drivers to take a break or rest – something about these cups struck me as remarkable and irritating: their size. I estimated the holding capacity of each at about ten liters – so huge that the entire shelf had place enough for only three of them. I wondered if they were joke articles, or supposed to store several weeks of supplies or actually meant for usage by people who frequently drove excessively overtired?

I myself once were offered a ride by a friendly but overtired road train driver – it was at night, he had been at the wheel for more than 24 hours already and was hoping that I would help to keep him awake by telling him stories. However since I had been up all day, soon after departing I fell asleep on the co-driver's seat. When I awoke some hours later to him still steering his road train at the maximum permitted speed, now however through pitch black night on a country road which was only lit up immediately ahead of us by the truck's headlights reflected by dense fog that wafted on the road like an endless series of gray stage curtains which were always whisked away before us at the very last moment, solely to reveal ever more of those curtains while

Make a conscious effort to make it back home alive and healthy!

keeping to hide whatever might've been standing in our way somewhere ahead of us.

Gravel roads

Gravel roads do exist. Some of them are major roads. Adjust your speed upon encountering one (usually there are signs to warn you in advance when you're about to). Driving on gravel slackens, disperses and throws stones into the air. Thus, keep significant distance from vehicles which are driving in front of you. In case a vehicle is coming on from the other direction, pull over to the side, stop completely and let it pass before you head on. Otherwise you'll hit the stones that the other vehicle throws in the air, and should a flying stone hit your car the speeds of both would sum up, thus increasing any damage done. Windows can break. So can bones. In the outback, cracked windshield are a frequent sight.

Car Bra. That's the brand name of car accessories fashioned from vinyl. Their function is to partially cover cars in order to protect their paint from scratches and other minor damages while driving. Caring for and tuning cars (including shelling out money to have them painted in flashy colors) is a favorite past-time of many Australians. Even if Car Bras are a sight that needs getting used to, they're applied very frequently because that's how frequent one encounters hazardous road conditions in Australia.

Road trains on gravel roads

Road trains rarely have any fenders. In case you encounter one on a gravel road, make way for it because it won't make way for you. Pull over to the side as far as you can, then stop and stay there until it's over. Road train's many wheels propel a lot of stones up into the air, and due to the missing fenders the first obstacle they'll encounter are your car and its windshield and (in the worst case) you.

On the road from Mount Isa to Three Ways, we met a road train. It was shortly after we had crossed over the border between Queensland and the Northern Territory and I had taken the helm. Ten kilometers prior to the meeting, the two-lane tarmac had ended, giving way to only one-lane tarmac accompanied on both sides by broad side-strips of gravel. Said road train was the first vehicle we encountered which came from the other direction on that stretch of road. It was driving exactly on the tarmaced strip in the center and didn't made any motion whatsoever from which one could conclude that its driver had any intentions to dodge from there by even as little as an inch. There was a very brief discussion in our car as to how we should act now. Consensus: It seemed too unlikely that the road train would dodge and it would certainly be much better (and beneficial) if we would – and soon! So I steered the car onto the gravel and continued to drive there at almost the same speed. When the road train started to pass us just seconds later, it kicked up dust – there suddenly was that much dust around us that it blackened out all daylight so thoroughly as if a foggy, moonless night had fallen from one second to the next. In any direction we could only see ahead for about two to three meters – beyond that, anything was veiled behind endlessly passing stampedes of brown and black curtains of dust. Black wheels without any fenders rolled fast past us through our area of vision, first a couple followed by dozens and soon I lost count while simultaneously noting they came in tightly closed rows. Each wheel was higher than our car and they passed us fast like a self-moving wall – like tumbling boulders dancing a polonaise within a massive stone avalanche –

like a queue of shoppers rushing with their trolleys to a cashier's desk about to open. The stones which the wheels tossed up in the air were flying like snowflakes in a dust-brown winter storm, everywhere around us and into all directions– like a panicking flock of granite gray birds just plunging up into the air to flee headless, just different as these things flying around weren't soft flakes or birds with minds and self preservation instincts, but solid, sharp stones that could damage or hurt with no regret or bad consciousness. Since during those long moments I kept the car driving at top speed, the sum of the speeds at which the stones and we were travelling would've been huge and quite damaging in case we would have collided. Luckily, this apocalypse went past soon; we had survived it undamaged and drove on into a new day with a cloudless blue sky while the road train disappeared in our rear view mirror as fast as it had appeared.

Animals on road / driving at night (and during the day)

Australia's landscape provides wild animals with plenty of wide open space traversed by very few roads with very little traffic. They're thus not accustomed to cars and have no idea about the damage animals and cars can inflict upon each other during an accident. Be prepared at any time to meet animals on the road which tread on it as if it was just another piece of landscape. Expect them to ignore you and your car as if you were invisible – even if just moments ago they had to witness how one of their mates got run over by a vehicle. Don't drive during twilight or at night at all, because that's when most animals will be awake and on the move. If you see one or several animals, stop and wait. They usually travel in groups – more of them will follow directly behind.

I really enjoyed driving the limousine I had rented out in Roma. It had a built-in cruise control function thanks to which the car could automatically keep cruising at a set velocity without requiring me to keep my foot on the speed pedal. That proved very comfortable for the long and uneventful drive through the outback. I had rented the car to travel to remote Carnarvon Gorge National Park (by the way: Almost all Australian national parks are remote from the remainder of the world. It's the same the other way around as well as among them) – a 250 kilometer drive each way. Thanks to the cruise control I just had to push a button and the car kept flying at the speed at which I was driving the moment I pushed the button. To achieve that, it sped up or slowed down all by itself. So I accelerated up to 100km/h, the maximum allowed speed, switched on the cruise control and then relaxed my legs, even folded them below me under the seat, while enjoying the view onto the red, shrub-spotted plain flying past left and right. It seemed much like I was sitting gemuetlich on a comfortable sofa and steered how the land was flying past. It felt like being a passenger in an airplane flying really close to the ground and free from all obstacles or distractions. Thus passed a while until eventually I spotted a black heap sitting on the road in my lane in some distance ahead of me. It occupied the entire lane with its broadness, was about a meter high and I was getting closer to it fast. I pulled my legs out from under me and started to push the brake pedal to slow down the car way before it (because of that, cruise control automatically deactivated itself). I rolled onwards slowly towards the black heap, ready to swerve around it or stop entirely. But while I were approaching – I still was a safe distance away from it – the heap dissolved into a group of black ravens which hopped away from each other spreading and fluttering with their wings; they jumped up into the air and flew away. The road was clear and no raven was to be seen anywhere at all before I arrived anywhere even remotely close to the spot in the road where they had sat together as a group. It took me a bit of time (and discomfort) until I had accelerated the car again and could turn on the cruise control again at the speed I wished to voyage at. With that completed all right I could again lean back, relax and enjoy the landscape fly past. A few kilometers onwards and some minutes later I encountered another black heap sitting in my lane. I hit the brake again (because of that cruise control automatically deactivated itself again). These black ravens, too, dissolved quickly from each other and flew away immediately. By the time that I passed trough the spot they had been sitting in, they had long cleared the lane which I was driving in. Again it cost me quite a bit of time and discomfort until I had gotten the car back up to speed so I could switch back on the cruise control, relax again and marvel at the landscape. The pattern in the bird's behavior looked very clear to me: Since they always flew away betimes, it wasn't necessary at all to break and lose the comfort by the automatic cruise control. And comfortable it was; it became even more obvious some kilometers further. There, the road went straight up a short, steep incline. I could hear the engine being revved up by the cruise control to keep the speed and feel the acceleration push me back into the seat. I were impressed – and found the cruise control even more handy for my comfort, enjoyment and relaxation. So when several minutes later upon again spotting another heap of black ravens sitting in my lane, I just kept careering forward at the same speed, expecting that these ravens would too dissolve and clear the road in time for me to pass through. However we were getting close to each other fast. But the ravens didn't move a single inch. So I had to brake hard, as hard as I could. It felt like putting the brakes to a thorough test. For a fraction of a second I wondered if this would go well – it was a matter of weal and woe – the car finally got to a standstill, mere centimeters away from the black, unshaped heap. Nothing happened for a second, then finally the huge black perentie rose. Across the hood it was barely visible; now that it got up the upper quarter of it came into view. It turned its head and looked at me for a moment, stuck out its tongue as if it was tasting the air, then looked ahead again towards the batter and trudged off the road, carried by its four short stumpy legs, its muscles clearly visible at work under its thick skin that was covered in anthracite-black scales. Another moment passed until until he had left, only then the road ahead was open for me again.

Something alike happened to me early one morning just outsides of Seymour. My workmates and me had driven the very same route for the past several weeks, shuttling between our places of residence and of employment twice a day. During our first run, it was always still night so pitch black as if light had never been made or even thought of – long before the onset of dawn. We had departed a rural town still soundly asleep and were driving into the surrounding countryside. As usual, I sat crammed into the backseat with three others, eating the breakfast I had brought – sandwiches, which I had prepared for myself the previous evening and kept in my fridge overnight so that I could sleep for a few precious minutes longer and, in case I would've overslept, not have to make my colleagues wait unnecessarily. So there I was, munching on toast with jam, halfway between being awake and being asleep and dreaming, not yet ready to speak (i.e., with the three people left and right of me who already were awake enough to engage in conversation); while two more colleagues were in place on the front seats ahead of me and (like parents) taking care of steering and the associated responsibility. Even further ahead of me two bright cones of light were visible which the car's headlamps unveiled like paper cut-outs out of the curtain night had pulled over road and landscape. I focused on my sandwich, because that moment everything else seemed comparably unimportant to me since after innumerous identical tours it appeared just as usual and already well-known to me. But suddenly the driver slammed on the brakes and brought the car to an abrupt halt. We were thrown forward into our buckles; I had to hold on tight to keep my precious jam sandwich from going to waste. Everyone but me jumped out immediately before I could even ask, let alone notice what was going on. Some of them came rushing back just about as sudden, but only to grab their cameras; they disappeared again past the front of the car sooner than I could arrange my thoughts and get them to take shape, formulate a coherent question and start to set my mouth into operation. Eventually (after finishing the last few bites of my sandwich) I, too, got out in order to find out just what was causing this upheaval. I found our car was standing in its lane flat out. In front of it (four meters away and floodlit by the headlamps) my workmates stood in a circle around the center of the road. As I drew nearer, I could finally make out what had made them stop: There, on the double yellow lines sat a koala bear and we stood around it in amazement, some of us being really excited at this find and some taking pictures. The koala on the other hand sat there looking back and up at us, seemingly entirely relaxed and at ease as if it was doing just that day in and day out. Somewhen, someone handed him a handful of eucalyptus leaves picked from one of the trees growing adjacent to the road, which he gladly accepted. He started to munch on them and remained seated as relaxed as a meditative Buddha despite bystanders taking pictures of him and further cars that passed him and us during those minutes. Only after several minutes had passed he leaned forward, bowed down on all fours and crawled off the road and beyond at the speed of a baby. A slow and furry baby which had no idea which danger it had put itself and us into.

Encountering an animal on the road doesn't always end that harmless. An acquaintance once gave me a ride in her car from Cooma to Wagga Wagga across the Snowy Mountains. We rushed through the forests at a speed of about 100 km / h – the trees which zipped past stood on either side of us like tall, massive and dark green walls and just like them time just seemed to fly. In the car among ourselves we talked about this and that and then a giant grey kangaroo all of a sudden appeared our lane, jumping into from left just three meters ahead of us, coming from somewhere left of the road looking ahead focused as if it hadn't noticed us – and it jumped on without stopping, taking with it a germinating inkling of sure and sudden death. It left the road as sudden as it had appeared. Lucky us – and lucky kangaroo! Because telling from its looks, it had been about 2.5 meters tall with a circumference to match – maybe about 200 kg heavy! We could only guess what had made it jump about so focused in broad daylight, and were grateful for having ridden out that situation alive and healthy. The son of another acquaintance however wasn't as lucky as we were; she gave me a lift on her way from Adaminaby to visit him at the Cooma hospital. En route, she stopped at the local garage to look at his car wreck. It was a barely recognizable heap of smashed metal.

Not all animals which pose a road hazard can move. Roo bars consist of solid metal. Their purpose is to warrant that the vehicles which bear them can keep moving after a collision. They're colloquially named after their purpose: roo is an abbreviation for kangaroo. Animals hurt or killed through being overrun are rarely buried, carried away or at least moved to the roadside – instead they're left lying around in the street where they died, posing a risk to your car, and making for a saddening sight.

Driving during twilight and at night
Here's a summary of abovementioned counter-arguments (and a new one): During twilight and at night there's increased risk of encountering nocturnal animals, drunk drivers, unlit vehicles and road trains not lit enough for you to estimate their dimensions. Road train drivers frequently overstep the driving period permitted by law and are overtired. Plus, there's nothing to see.

I travelled from Port Augusta to Coober Pedy and back on overnight long distance bus lines. It was around the new moon. Purportedly that region is very scenic, but the only thing I could see outsides was just pitch black – which tellingly is the name of a movie filmed in that region.

Unfenced roads
Roads secured with guard rails are rare in Australia. These even are missing besides of steep, winding roads that run along cliffs and scarps. Adjust your speed accordingly.

Complete with signatures, the messages "Steven, we love you!" and "Steven, you're our best friend!" are spray-painted in lime green onto two huge boulders which line a steep and narrow road that winds down from the Atherton Tablelands. That road has no protection from the precipice immediately adjacent to it – neither shoulder nor banquette, no guard rails and no catch fences. The aforementioned two messages are followed by one on a third boulder. It reads: "Steven, we miss you!"

As I was told, the road leading up to Blackdown Tableland National Park is even more dangerous: slippery and muddy after rain – and on top of that it's in constant use by heavy log trucks. So I was told in Rockhampton from which I had intended to set out to visit that park. I were about to rent a car as that park (like most other parks) isn't served by public transport. The rental car office to which I turned was located at the local airport which only handles regional and domestic flights, thus sporting a rather small terminal. This rental car company was the sole one which had a counter there. When I stepped into the small terminal hall of steel and black marble, it lay quiet and almost deserted – despite the rental agent and me nobody was there. I happened to stumble upon her desk right after entering from landside as it was located immediately adjacent to the door. So I inquired about my reservation, were handed the forms necessary and just when I had filled and signed them all and were ready to hand them over to get the car, a couple came strolling into the terminal which otherwise still lay quiet. The agent immediately struck up a conversation with them, seemingly surprised and delighted at the sight of attendants – utterly unawaited. As she told them, since no departures or arrivals were scheduled for the next couple of hours. So she asked them for the reason why they arrived at this time. When they explained their reasons, it turned out that their story partially overlapped with mine: This couple had travelled to the airport from a town up the very road which led past the national park where I was intending to go. They had arrived way too early for their holiday flight because due to severe weather en route, they had set off from their home town with extensive time buffer.

However, all had went much better than feared and they were considering themselves very lucky. When the rental agent took note of and pointed out to us that they had taken the road I intended to travel on, she asked them for road conditions and mentioned my plans – and the couple immediately turned to me and strongly advised me against going on that journey because of these adverse conditions (they had experienced similar first-hand earlier). As they said, making matters worse was that they had seen (and knew) the access road that led up to the park when driving past its turnoff. Based on their observation and know-how, they described in vivid detail fallen trees, heavy downpours that turned the muddy road into a slippery slope as well as neck-breaking opposing traffic consisting mostly of log trucks – and that in this weather the access road to the park could only be driven in a 4WD which in turn required a skilled and experienced driver (whereas I had opted to hire a car of the smallest and cheapest category available, believing that acting so would save me money). The agent joined the two in talking me out of my plans even though that meant she would forgo my business. Together they managed to persuade me to not go at all – much to the delight of the agent, who (while she was manually shredding the paperwork) that otherwise she would've had to deny letting me a car for the sake of my own well-being and the rental car staying in running condition.

No infrastructure

On main roads rest stops can usually be found about every 150 to 200 kilometers. In case distances are longer, signage ahead expressively warns about it. Minor roads aren't blessed with them either. Check ahead what you might find and carry supplies for whatever you need on the way. This is a good idea for safety as well as for financial reasons: Some rest stops charge horrendous prices, claiming sky-high costs for having trucked them in. Here, being self-sufficient pays immediately and significantly, even if you're solely commuting from one town to another on only paved roads – that is: on the very last indications you can hold on to out there in the wide open Outback landscape that prove to you while you're en route through it that somewhere beyond the horizon a highly civilized world exists.

Staying at night

All around the country there are hotels, motels, youth hostels and campgrounds. The latter ones can be found insides and outsides of national parks; some of them charge a fee while many are free to stay. There are guidebooks and websites available which give directions and list what facilities they feature (free campgrounds usually offer no food vending, guards, showers or running tap water). Make sure to arrive before sunset at the campground of your choice as finding them and pitching camp in the black of the night is difficult or impossible.

Free campgrounds can be in very remote areas. If you prefer not to camp alone, a simple way to find others for safety in numbers is to simply stay at a commercial campground where you'll find plenty of others who likewise prefer to keep company.

To keep animals out of your vehicle, keep doors and windows closed at all times, lock away any foodstuff (including leftovers) and keep your car free of anything ants might find savory.

Locals like to play it safe when staying in free campgrounds – or so a few Australians (usually members of senior generations) told me when I mentioned to them my plans about overland travel.

According to their advice, when driving overland it'd be a good idea to frequent rest stops immediately besides the roads for staying over night, making sure to arrive there long before the sun sets – and then firstly remain firmly seated inside the car with doors locked and windows shut – there, one should wait until at least two other travel parties would arrive for likewise staying over night so that there are enough strangers to keep watch over each other. If however only one or none other travel parties arrive, one should eventually give up waiting, restart the engine and drive on until the next rest stop, repeating this until one has found at least two other parties for camping together. This I were told on various occasions, eke by several tent neighbors on campgrounds subject to a charge; yet they themselves only knew the idea from hearsay decades ago and when questioned detected that they had never actually tried.

Both being in good company and having observers present can rid you of worry and fear while camping. Yet when travelling with a new acquaintance – whom I had made through another acquaintance and never met before setting off together in his car – our stop on the first evening was a remote and deserted campground somewhere in the woods of Kakadu National Park. It was very dark there even for the late hour; the full moon was being the sole source of light after he had killed the engine. We were forlorn and alone – even on the last few kilometers leading there not a single soul was to be seen hanging around anywhere among the dense forest. It was dead silent all around – not even animals could be heard; each sound we made could be heard so clearly in the deafening silence as if it had been massively amplified. The campground featured an iron hut furnished with modern and well-kept sanitary facilities – large enough to gulp and keep dozens of people at once. But it too was void of people and only lit by rays of moonlight filtering in through a single small window in the extensive roof area of corrugated sheet iron; that made the shadows even darker and turned the spaces afar from said window into eerie black holes that almost gravitated one forward into forlorn and eternal nothingness. Not even spiders had been dwelling in that hut as if they were avoiding the place – as if a crime scene cleaning crew had only just thoroughly scrubbed the entire place, then vanished into thin air the very second that we had turned around the last corner and showed up. That made the place even more deserted and lonely. After brushing my teeth in near-darkness, trying to avoid the black hole next to the washbasin, I set out to pitch up our tents which were stored in the back of my new travel mate's station wagon. Since I hadn't taken a look into the boot I didn't knew for sure what sat waiting in there – yet. That space was crammed to the rafters with the luggage of my travel mate solely. He had told me a bit about the tents and the other stuff on the morning of that very day when he introduced himself and his car upon our first brief face-to-face meeting. Following that meeting I had jumped aboard without even considering whether or not I should worry if that was a good idea - and we headed off. Looking at the boot's content from the front seat or through the windows I could make out a few pieces of it, but apart from that this accumulation appeared to me like a hidden tomb nobody had ventured into in aeons. To open a rear door to this secret vault for the first time felt like walking down the staircase into the basement of a deserted haunted house. So there I was – in the abandoned moonlit camp ground with nobody else around near or far, alone with a man I knew next to nothing about, reaching for the door handle to face the masses of gear he owned and had brought. The door squeaked in its hinges. And there, lying before me ready to hand was an ax! My face went bloodless and immediately I reclosed the door. My travel mate, standing at the opposite side of the car, caught sight of my frightened mien, inquired as to what was up and was kind and empathic enough to remove it the very second I explained my observation, even asking for apologies for him having scared me unintentionally. During our further journey, it turned out why he owned and brought such a tool: He was a talented cook and was travelling with a full camping kitchen equipment – it was extensive enough to cater for an entire travel group! He prepared us many haute cuisine meals on our journey in the wild; some of them cooked over an open log fire which he built with the help of his ax.

Here's a list of animals I found insides of cars: a giant huntsman spider a-hunting, a smacking possum feeding on food I owned and had been looking forward to eat just moments later, an ant trail leading straight through the intestines of a fully laded car.

Crap maps

So called "mud maps" are available for free all around Australia from tourist information desks, hotel receptions and national park information centers. They're only to serve as general information and their quality and dependability varies greatly – from rough sketches to professionally done layouts. Be warned: rarely any of them are to scale and they may contain errors and omissions.

I once drove with a rental car to go see a glowworm colony in a cave on the outskirts of the hilly, tree-covered range that is Lamington National Park. I had gotten myself a mud map from the Surfers Paradise tourist information. It was professionally designed and printed, contained lots of advertisements for local businesses and included the very spot I now wanted to travel to, displaying its location close to the edge of the map. I had made good experiences with said mud map as it had had proven to be reliable when I was visiting the city center, so I kept to trusting it and using it for orientation, unsuspecting of what was about to befall me. In order to be able to drive with both hands on the wheel and my eyes on the road, for the comparably longer drive away from the city I counted the number of turnoffs and bends on the way leading to my goal and then memorized and navigated by that. Soon, I reached the hilly area and drove amidst a lush green forest left, right and above of me; according to the mud map here the road was leading through the national park. I passed all of the turnoffs I had counted on the map but the last one. After the second last, for quite some time no more turnoffs came on. I grew tense with impatience because according to the map the turnoff I needed to take was supposed to turn up soon. However, instead and all of a sudden the forest and hills ended and gave way to open sky and agricultural lands. They were flat and no turnoff could be seen for the next couple of kilometers. I figured I had just left the national park and must have missed my turnoff within it, so I slowed down feeling at a loss as to what to do – and at that very moment I spotted a small house that sat nestled within the border of the forest among the very last trees. Quite a surprise – considering hat the next town was dozens of kilometers away. But apparently it was not an illusion yet still looked solid upon second look. It kept aloof from the road by about thirty meters and was fended off by a closed metal gate. I pulled over, parked the car in front of the gate and got out. Silence came and fell over me like a blanket. I took a look around. There wasn't anybody to be seen anywhere. Not a single thing was moving; it was as if the entire world was playing musical statues and the music just had stopped and so had everybody and everything except for me because I hadn't been informed yet as to what was happening. I yelled out a tentative hello towards the house, and then another one with more courage after getting to hear my own voice and finding out that (contrary to my doubts) during those moments sound had not ceased to exist and seemingly the world had not stopped turning after all – and just when I were about to give up (due to nothing happening) and simply retrace my steps, the front door opened and out stepped a woman, seemingly irritated at the stranger turning up and yelling at her front door. She shouted a reply towards me, inquiring about why I had called. Since she didn't even set a foot down from her doorstep, I had to engage with her in an entirely yelled conversation; starting with – to alleviate her obvious irritation about my motives, her apparently being fully alone out here – assuring her about my peaceful intentions as a lost traveller in dire need of directions from a local. The woman eventually decided to act helpful and with her advice aided me to get back on track: I simply needed to drive back up the hills and return to the turnoff I had counted as second last – about two kilometers back. Lucky me I had stopped and asked for directions – had I just driven on without thinking, I might have gotten lost entirely.

Buying a car or having a car serviced
Watch out not to get ripped off.

A brown station wagon sits besides the overland road near Camooweal – from there into both directions it's a very long drive to the nearest places, Mount Isa and Avon downs. It's abandoned and all its windows were smashed in. On its side, spray-painted black lettering states: "Just another stupid backpacker". It was the best-looking one of all the abandoned cars that I passed in Australia.

Winter

When driving in winter in the Australian alps, on most major roads law requires you to bring snow chains of appropriate size for your car's tires. Violations are dearly punished because this is for your own safety: Storms blowing in from nearby Antarctica transport with them clouds full of snow which they dump gladly and frequently onto the landscape, burying it under several meters high snow covers – sometimes going about this fervently from dusk til dawn and back without any end in sight. Roads do get cleared, but road maintenance vehicles only set out from their depots after the snow has stopped falling. And since the roads are dozens of kilometers long, since depots are located in the towns which lie widely dispersed and since it takes the vehicles some time to pave the way for themselves, it takes a while until the roads are cleared from fresh snowfall.

Authorities recommend to prepare well when driving in winter and thus bring further supplies: warm clothes, snow shovel, hot drinks, warm blankets and a full tank. They advise: Stay with the car in case of an emergency, because even if stuck it provides insulation from cold and wind and you can let the engine run for the heating as long as there is fuel left. Further people on their own are easily overlooked from road maintenance vehicles when they pass and rush through whereas cars aren't. By the way, in case you've been out in the cold for too long and suddenly feel so hot that you register an urge to throw off your clothes: It's actually the opposite, so stay dressed and urgently take care of warming yourself up!

I once waited at the city limit of Jindabyne for the public bus to Perisher. It was the beginning of the ski season and the weather was late-autumnal. The bus stop was an unprotected spot in the middle of a large, gravel-covered space that extended from the road on one side until the border of the forest on the other. Said place offered a panoramic view across the town and the barrier lake, but there wasn't any shelter that could have protected me from the weather which constantly alternated back and forth between sunshine and cold rain like a swingboat in full motion. When finally the bus pulled over, I had long both been soaked until my skin and gotten sunburnt.

Punctuality in public transport

Buses, ferries and trains always depart punctual in Australia, thanks to Australian timetables which incorporate generous time buffer for the absorption of any possible delays. Punctual departures are considered so important in Australian transport that when travelling on a route with connections, passengers are only permitted to book those where there's at least a total of sixty minutes between scheduled arrival of the feeder and departure of the connection in order to ensure that all passengers with bookings are present and ready to go at the scheduled departure time (even if this rule forces you to abstain from travelling on a connection which leaves just mere minutes after you came in on time with a feeder that arrives on schedule and on the very same platform – even if it forces you into a layover because on that very day there are no further connections departing your way). So, be there on time, or else one would depart without you and you've got to see to it yourself. Further, passengers are expected to take the lead and make themselves be identified as such. Buses in use for public transport usually carry a sign on their front that states "Signal Driver" – because you either indicate to the drivers that you want to journey with them or else they won't recognize that and won't stop for you.

I felt a bit dreamy when I was deboarding a ship in the port of Hervey Bay. For what had felt like an eternity, the ship had taken the other passengers and me really close to whales which were staying in the bay – it had been the first time in my life that I had seen these unfathomably large animals – out there on the water, they had appeared immediately next to the ship as sudden as they then had disappeared. Their wet, black and white skin had glinted in the sun. With their tiny black eyes they were observing us humans, seemingly as fascinated, curious and enjoying it as us excited people on the boat. Now that we were back again on shore, I just followed the crowd – my head was still in the clouds and my legs still were a bit wobbly, I don't know if that came from the fact that I had been on a ship for hours or from the experience. I had arrived to the port on a bus tour because it had been the sole transport option to get there. My hotel was situated in the greater Hervey Bay area, a one and a half hour drive away from the port. There simply wasn't any other transport mode available to get from hotel to port and back. Swimming with the swarm of humans, I wondered: At what time the bus might depart to carry us back? The crowd was moving towards the bus stop and the short way there led through a souvenir shop. Among the people walking ahead of me I made out a few people that I had seen sitting in the same bus as me on the way there; they started to browse around the shop. Apparently, there was still some time until departure. So, there I stood – in the midst of an avalanche of wale-related postcards, posters, fridge magnets and other souvenir trinkets – and my mind drifted back into vivid daydreams about what I had just experienced, about my still torrid brand-new memories.

Make a conscious effort to make it back home alive and healthy!

Because of that I overlooked how the shop emptied out. When finally I startled from my daydreams to the realization that quite some time had went past, that I had been alone in the shop for a while now and that everybody but me had walked out, I went straight for the exit through which my real eyes had seen people go while my inner eye had watched whales again and again. I were still uninformed about departure times of the tour bus and hoping for the best when I walked the last few steps to where the bus had dropped us off and gotten parked, yet it was nowhere to be seen. Had it been moved? I craned my neck to look into every corner of the parking lot twice, but the whole thing was as empty as blank paper sheets and abandoned people's hearts – the bus had left without me. I called the booking office on my mobile to inquire how I now might return to my hotel nonetheless. The person on the other end of the line was quite concerned about my situation and promised to immediately take care of solving it and call me back in a moment. And so it was: A few minutes later the same person called – now less flustered than before – and assured me that the bus would return, explaining that those conducting the bus had left without me because they had been believing that the group of passengers was complete and hadn't spotted me insides the shop – however, it would take some time until the bus would've returned. And so it did – I had to wait for almost an hour, since the bus had already been quite some distance away when the news about the one left behind had gotten through, and then it had taken even some more time until an opportunity to turn the bus around for heading back had been found.

I once booked a visit to the underwater lookout that sits in the water a couple dozen meters away from the main beach of Great Keppel Island. To get there, I were sold a ticket for a shuttle boat at the hotel reception, along with instructions for boarding: wait on the main beach at eight in the morning; the shuttle boat would come there to pick me up and bring me to the lookout. So the next morning, I stood bare-footed on the sand under the palm trees at the top of the beach, surveying the water for what might come. At the time scheduled, only the three ferry catamarans which connect the island to the mainland showed up – they rushed to the shore in a row (like people marching shoulder to shoulder – or better said: running, considering their velocity), threw down their gangways, dumped their load and sped off again like a Bondi tram – there and gone in under a minute (in doing so they gave the lookout the go-by). But no shuttle boat turned up. And on the ferries, no sign or boat crew had been visible which might've marked it as the shuttle boat. Nobody called out for me in specific or at least announced in general a trip towards the lookout. I waited there under the palm trees, assuming that the shuttle was late, keeping my eyes on the water and thus on the entry to the lookout that laid above water – so close and yet out of reach. Five uneventful minutes passed without any boat showing up or anything else happening; they stretched into fifteen minutes during which absolutely nothing happened (except for row after row of little surging billows swashed ashore) and melted into an endless eternity of thirty minutes in a lonely uniformity on an eternally identical sun-drenched postcard picture beach. Then I gave up, shook the sand off my feet and made my way straight over to the hotel reception where I had purchased the ticket. There, I was told to my surprise that one of the three ferries which I had seen was actually doubling as the shuttle boat. Subsequently I were asked for my ticket, so I handed it over and surprisingly were given a fresh one in return for a trip on the following day. Now, that day almost brought a deja vu – there I was again on the main beach, but instead of waiting among the palm trees I proactively walked towards the three ferries which again came running in like on the day before. But which one of them was the right one? I hastily approached the one on the right as it was closest to me; by the time I had run to the water's edge all ferries were already done dumping their modicum of passengers. Like before, on the deck there wasn't a sign or crew member present to provide information whether this was the shuttle boat, so I spontaneously decided to go search for a crew member. I jumped onto the gangway and walked up, hurrying so much (since I knew from the day before how soon all of the ferries would withdraw from the shore and leave) that I tripped over almost every single one of the bumps in the aluminum plank lying flat which actually were built into it to increase its usability when standing steep. I entered the ship's interior (it was constructed as one large glazed round room sitting atop of two hulks) – and addressed the first crew member I bumped into: Was this the ferry that doubled as shuttle boat to the underwater lookout? No, he replied, it was the one over there. With that, he waved vaguely towards the windows on one side. I turned my head and looked into the direction of his gesture – the windows gave view onto both of the other ferries, one behind the other. I thus had to ask: Which one – was he maybe referring to the one next to us – and I asked again and a third time until he had turned back to me and heard me over the engine noise (by that time the ferry closer to us was pulling up its gangway) – and when he did that vague gesture again (twice), I had to keep asking until I finally got a precise answer out of him: No, it was the far one. By now, that one was pulling back from the shore and turning to depart for the open sea, closely followed by the one closer to us. There I stood, flabbergasted about the fact that again I had missed the shuttle due to lack of information – only to be addressed immediately by that crew member next to me – did I intend to go with them on their boat to the mainland? If so, could I present my ticket for checking or else would I purchase one now? In the latter case I would have to pay cash since they couldn't accept credit cards on the boat. If however I did not wanted to depart with them, I would have to disembark on the spot since the boat was supposed to be leaving immediately – actually not now, but several moments ago already if it hadn't been for me holding them up.

Initially I had intended to only stay for two days in the camping place adjacent to the Jondaryan sheep shearing shed, but the place was so laid-back that I stayed double as long. When finally I checked out at the reception office, crew members asked me about my onwards travel plans. These were quite simple as I owned a bus travel pass: board the next available long distance bus. That plan only had one flaw: I had no idea as to when the next bus would depart. Crew members offered to check the timetable for me and found that there were only five minutes left until the next departure (and that this town saw a total of only two departures per day)! One of them offered to drive me to the bus stop, which I gladly accepted. We threw us and my luggage into her 4WD, hurtled and trundled down an unpaved piste (actually a side road of the main road which, in contrast to the piste, was one of those well developed overland roads; it led so straight through town as if it had been drawn with a ruler). We managed to arrive at the bus stop two minutes prior to the scheduled departure time. I jumped out with my luggage, said thank-you and goodbye and waited impatiently at the kerb, expecting the bus to arrive at any moment. To no avail – no bus showed up. After a couple minutes of nothing happening, I worriedly gathered my gear and lugged it and myself towards the rest station which laid across the road from the bus stop in order to ask for the whereabouts of the bus. I crossed the stations' parking place and entered its cafe – a place which looked like it came straight from the 1950s. It was endowed with a twenty meters long floor to ceiling glass front which gave a panoramic view of a large section of the road. You could actually watch how vehicles were approaching, driving past and getting smaller again as they were heading for the horizon. At the counter of the cafe I explained what had happened (or better said: not happened). In reaction, the woman behind the counter immediately reached out for a telephone to contact the bus company about what was up with the bus. She was still dialing when from the corner of my eye I spotted a familiar blur of color: It was the color unique to the long distance buses of which I had been awaiting one. Puzzled, I turned around to the windows. And then I could only stand there and watch in IMAX-like panorama how the bus which I had expected came closer and then careered past the place. Initially I felt surprised and baffled – then desperate as to what I could do about it (since it was too late by now for grabbing my luggage and attempting to run with it to the bus stop) – then hopeful at the thought that perhaps the bus might halt for other passengers. However, this was a stop on demand (registered through prior reservation or waving down the bus at the bus stop) and since neither me nor anybody had made a reservation for this town or could signal the driver from the completely deserted bus stop, all I could do was watch disillusioned how the bus drove across the whole width of the panorama and then left the picture at its other end, gone again in under a minute. The woman behind the counter told the person who had taken her call that it had been dealt with and that the bus she was about to inquire about had shown up; then she put down the receiver and just looked at me pitying.

This ends the section on dangers when en route. Now, what if you decide to not travel by yourself? Well, you might book a guided tour. Or you could team up with other travellers. The next section deals with the risks of doing the latter.

Getting around – travelling with others

travelling together with others might seem like a good idea when considering only the financial aspects. But there are plenty of downsides which arising from your potential co-travellers themselves:

their personality
What is a person like when you're together 24 hours each day, several days on end? That's how long it takes at least to cross even a minor bit of Australia. Within just a few days, all the masks would have come down and people will stop hiding how they really are. It's difficult to leave a party travelling together in the outback even if you urgently wanted to: Is the next town served by a bus connection? And if you jump out to get rid of them on the spot: How would you travel onwards from the middle of nowhere, far away from civilization? Would someone pass by, stop and pick you up from there (that's to say not just anybody but someone well-meaning)?

Two friends travelling together that I've made at a rodeo had been colleagues at work. For five years they had undergone an apprenticeship in a mountain hotel with shared accommodation for all the crew members. They knew that working and lodging with many others was totally different from constantly being alone together and around each other within the confined space of a caravan – it might have happened that they had to face the fact that they weren't getting along well. For that case they had discussed and agreed on an alternative plan: sell the jointly bought caravan and go separate ways. They mentioned to me several times how they considered themselves lucky that their initial plan was working well.

It didn't work well for three Québécois and me. They repeatedly made a point of not being "crazy Canadians", but proudly boasted they were "really crazy Québécois". We set off from Perth towards Adelaide and only made it there with a lot of tightly clenched teeth, throwing silent yet angry looks and by arranging overnight stays in hotels at different ends of towns through which we passed.

their driving

Road conditions in Australia are different from those at the place you're from – wherever that might be. Are you experienced and confident enough to take your driving skills to Australian roads? Are you confident enough to sit calmly in a car when somebody else has a go?

One and a half days after setting out from Melbourne in a large rental car with three acquaintances, we finally got to drive on the first goal of our tour: the Great Ocean Road. But immediately after driving through the first bend, we were stopped by a police car. It had been driving in the opposite direction, had passed us and then instantly turned around and signaled us to halt at a stopping bay. The police officer who got out of said car was really furious. Our driver lowered her window through which he almost shouted at her his demand to see her papers, spit flying from his mouth. She, a nineteen-year-old from Denmark, jumped out shocked, sprinted to the boot and rummaged among our luggage to find her license – her facial expression a combination of: worry, shock and concern having a flamboyant rave party together. The police officer stood besides her and looked on for a moment – his lips pressed together, his eyes concealed behind sunglasses – then he seemed to realize something and change his point of view. He switched his supporting leg and relaxed his pose which was quite a contrast to his voice when he started to speak again a moment later. Now, his tone was even sharper and stricter than before. He lectured her about what he had had to witness when we had driven through the bend and what likely consequences thereof were: In the bend, the gargantuan limousine which we had been assigned at the car rental had driven across and beyond the solid line – into his lane in the very moment when he had passed us. He looked like he was foaming with anger, yet it really appeared like he was hoping to drive home a lesson to an inexperienced driver young enough to be reachable. Finally, he left without fining us, mentioning he did so on purpose and explaining that he hoped he had been able to teach us something. After he had driven off, we had to calm down our driver. We supported her in digesting shock, confusion and hurt feelings, understanding the lesson and restrengthening her trust in her driving skills to give her back the sentiment she really could control a car this huge (for both of that I even walked around the entire car keeping close to it, so she could watch from the mirrors and most accurately imprint on her memory where the ends of the limousine were). Later on the road she told me of danish highways which until then had been the only country roads she had collected hands-on experience with: spacious and straight, multi-lane and single-direction highways as are typical for Europe. Try finding that in Australia – here's hint so you can recognize them more easily: Because they're so rare ,every few kilometers signs explain their correct use, stating "no bicycles allowed".

their intentions
Can you really trust a stranger? A well-meaning friend once advised me: "The only person you can really trust is you yourself – and then there's no one for a long distance – and then, far away, there are your parents" – those people who unconditionally paved the way for you into this world.

By chance I met an acquaintance in Adelaide. It was our first face-to-face encounter; before that we had only conversed via phone. Our contact had begun months ago when I found a notice she had posted on a blackboard of an Alice Springs hostel and until then had entirely taken place via a couple of rushed phone calls every now and then. Now that for the first time we were talking in person and without the pressure of having to pay per minute spoken, we found out that by chance we had taken the same route, passing through Darwin, Exmouth, Broome and Perth independently from each other, with her always about two weeks ahead of me. And upon comparing our travel experiences in more detail we found out that each of us two (again independently from each other) had travelled the east coast of Queensland and had crossed paths with a third traveller. Than man had offered – both to her and to me – to journey through the Outback together with him, albeit with one significant difference in his offering: To me he had offered private quarters in his tent which he would've borrowed to me during the journey whereas he would've slept in the back of his station wagon. To her he never mentioned a tent but instead proposed for her to lodge in his car – repeatedly, until eventually she understood what he was trying to convey, declined on the spot and never met him again.

Others weren't that lucky and ended up in newspaper headlines which they'll never be reading themselves. Their stories have been made into movies – scary horror movie dramas.

I once heard about a hitchhiker who tried to travel by hitchhiking and actually had someone stop for him (supposedly this is an urban legend – neither sane nor insane persons would hitchhike in Australia). It was a car with a camper in tow. The people in the car told him to put his backpack into the camper due to too few space in the car. When he had done so and was on his way back to the car in order to get in, the driver suddenly accelerated and the people drove away and left the tourist in the outback with no water and no way to call for help.

their insurance coverage

Almost anytime I were on the road with friends or acquaintances, it happened that at one time or another an animal would cross our path and just barely miss us. In case there would've been an accident, would their insurance have covered any damage to my property and to me?

if you want to get rid of them...

... how would you move onwards? On most roads there's little to no traffic. And it's an entirely different question if somebody would pick you up at all. Because in the outback someone standing around (far away from any witnesses) could be malicious.

Even on major Australian roads traffic is actually as sparse as the clichés tell. Even on major roads with no alternative routing the music is over before you see somebody pass – I can tell because I tried: En route from Roma to Injune I wanted to exchange the music CD playing in the car stereo. However I didn't manage to drive, handle the CDs and handle the (to me new and thus unaccustomed) car stereo all at the same time. Making it even more difficult was the fact that there wasn't a single possibility to stop coming up: The road had no shoulder, no cutout and on top of it all the road lay half a meter lower than the area left and right – I could've literally pushed up the daisies while driving by if there had been any. Now, what were I going to do? I looked ahead at the road void of oncoming traffic and that's when I remembered a newspaper article on driving in Australia which I had read years ago – and an idea formed in my mind. In that article, a ride with a local driver in the outback was described. The driver was quoted as complaining (I've no idea whether he was serious or kidding) about the masses of oncoming traffic after having met just two cars in one hour. Thus my idea was this: Stop right where I were: in the middle of the road so that I would have both hands free to properly switch the CDs. I checked the mirrors: There was no traffic to be seen in front of or behind me. I decelerated from 100km/h to standstill, then switched the music while constantly keeping an eye on the road into both directions. No other cars were coming while I was working fast and focused. When finally the new music came on I realized I could stay put in peace and calm for a few more moments, so I slowly took in the road and the scenery around me for the sole and for the last time while standing there, feeling joyous that my idea had worked out well. Then I drove on. While making the first couple of meters, I wondered for how long I could have sat there without disturbing anybody. To find out, I paid attention to observe just how much time would pass until I met another car. It was only after a total drive of

30 minutes that I encountered another vehicle coming from the other direction. Had I sat where I switched the CDs (disregarding any traffic that might have been moving in the same direction as I did) the music would've long finished until I'd seen another car.

That's been it with warnings and bad stories from me. Let's finish with my good stories that really are worth being told and remembered, in order to encourage you to go travelling yourself – because if you dare and prepare well, you can make your own good stories and create memories that will elate you for the rest of your life.

3. THE GOOD STORIES

If you leave it all behind, it'll stay there waiting for you to return

My electric shaver runs on rechargeable battery – and once when I departed Melbourne I forgot to pack the charging cable and left it behind in a youth hostel dorm room. I only took notice five days later and quite a distance apart. By the time my travel itinerary led me back there I had grown a beard. Nonetheless reception staff recognized me at once – they even complimented me for my (rather involuntary) new look. I inquired for the charging cable and they checked their lost and found box – to no avail; it wasn't in there. It hadn't been found. I started to bother about consequences thereof, but the receptionists who had checked the box sat it down and in one swift motion grabbed a room key, turned to head off for the dorm room and asked me to follow close behind. She let me into the room and encouraged me to search for the cable myself. I found it straightaway: It was still plugged into the power strip where I had last used it. That dorm room had constantly been fully occupied. Seemingly all of the patrons which had stayed there since my departure must have been believing that my cable was property of another sojourner, and thus left it untouched.

Upon departing from North Stradbroke Island, I was waiting at the bus stop. Just across the road from me stood the small hotel at which I had stayed and relaxed for a couple of days. Directly behind it I could make out the sandy beach and the ocean. Next to me stood my luggage – a large backpack and two small bags, all of it freshly hand-packed by me myself. While I was standing there with the faint sound of rolling waves in my ear and my eyes resting on my gear and my thoughts just drifting here and there a question dawned on me: Hadn't there once been more gear with me – didn't I additionally possess a green sleeping bag? If so, where was it? Exactly that moment the little local bus, all painted green, rolled in, keeping me from starting to worry about or look around for the sleeping bad. The lid of its trailer was opened so that I could load my luggage, and exactly then and there right before my nose was lying my sleeping bag which I had forgotten three days ago when exiting at this very stop upon arrival to the hotel and which I hadn't missed since. I gladly mentioned that to the driver who completely indifferently explained to me how her kids had suggested they remove it from the trailer, which she refused. Her reason for that: Leaving lost and found items in the bus was – both logically as well as according to her own experience – the most effective measure to return them to their owners, because on Straddie there only exists one bus line, with only one bus, driven by this very driver – and every visitor to the island voyages with them at least twice.

Free water everywhere

You can get drinking water for free everywhere, even in the outback. Sole preconditions are that you ask for it and bring your own bottle. I experienced that many times, including at the Threeways roadhouse where café staff told me to help myself from a tap just straight out the door. But dangling from the sole tap I found there was a small hand-painted warning sign, advising that I better: "Don't drink from this tap". Adding to the repudiative impression it gave was the fact that the water-tap sat atop a metal tube which stuck out of the lawn adjacent to the petrol station, so I assumed it wouldn't give off potable but just service water for irrigation. So I returned into the station's café to ask for better directions to the tap which they had in mind. There at the counter, I started into a short report of what I had found, yet got interrupted immediately with a reassurance: Yes, that was the very tap they had been talking about and they had put up that sign solely to discourage road train drivers from connecting it to their water tanks and help themselves to several hundred liters of water. So then I returned outsides and held my water bottles under that tap and helped myself to 4 liters.

There is such thing such as a free lunch!

And it's quite simple to obtain. Just position yourself in a hostel communal room around lunch or dinner time. Sooner or later, a few young men will emerge from the adjacent kitchen. One of them will carry a large pot of tomato sauce and another one a pan full of spaghetti – amounting to much more food than this small group could eat in an entire day, let alone in one sitting. They'll be setting it down on a table, fetch cutlery and crockery from the kitchen and then they'll sit down and feed themselves from the spaghetti mountains and the red sauce sea. However, even though they'll be helping themselves to seconds and thirds and fourths (even when they're visibly stuffed) they're unable to noticeably erode the spaghetti ranges or part the red sea. Finally, they'll lock eyes, nod each to other to signal that they agree to give up, then rise from their chairs and carry the whole enchilada back to the kitchen with an air of frustration. Now you must jump into action, give up your observation post and act quick and decisively! Follow them into the kitchen! Because these are young men who were never taught how to cook. Now that they're away from home for the very first time and in need to prepare themselves food on their own, their mothers have told them on the phone that cooking was quite simple – and how to do it (watered down version to convey over the phone to the unillumined): Purchase one jar of tomato sauce and one pack of spaghetti, then prepare both according to what it says on the packaging. What wasn't mentioned in that guidance was that the amount prepared should be sized according to the number of eaters – and how any leftovers could be stored. So, when you've rushed after them into the kitchen, you'll encounter them looking regretfully and bent over the trash bin, about to throw away all the leftover food. Just ask them "Do you still want to eat that?" and immediately they'll step back from the bin and turn to you. Merriment and happiness will suddenly shine from their faces (like like sunbeams breaking through storm clouds) and their arms will extend forward and hold out the food towards you (in a wide gesture that looks as if they feel like giving you a hug out of gratefulness for saving them from throwing away their self-cooked meal), long before they've managed to exclaim in an overjoyed, this-is-almost-too-good-to-be-true tone (stumbling over their own words, in broken, heavily accented English) a question that is rather rhetoric because their arms already said it: "Do you want?" So there's your free lunch! Enjoy! (And while I'm at it: Thanks again for the food to dozens of young men – and their moms!)

The Australian Way of dealing with answering machines

Australians have an especially polite way of leaving messages on voice mailboxes – or so I used to believe. I initially gained that impression after having shared my Australian mobile phone number with many locals. Every time that I had missed a call and an Australian left me a message, they always formulated them with plenty of politeness and formality. At the start of the messages,

Make a conscious effort to make it back home alive and healthy!

the callers always mentioned their full names. They then stated that the message about to follow was meant for me (always giving my precise and full name) and only then they gave the actual message, closing with a mention of a phone number where they were reachable for a return call. I felt quite glad and excited to have discovered such a unique cultural quirk and to be spoilt with such polite treatment over and over again. 'Til one day on which, following me having received and listened to another one of those sincerely polite messages, I started to wonder if maybe this wasn't an unusual quirk of common polite behaviour unique to Australia culture. Could it possibly be due to other reasons – was it maybe just a reaction to the announcement of the voice mailbox? That sounded plausible to me since I had purchased my prepaid mobile phone from a traveller who was about to fly back home to Belgium. According to the phone's manual its voice mailbox had a standard announcement as well as the option to record a personal one (which I had never done). The moment those thoughts were careering through my head I was walking down a road in the Sydney city center and my eyes feel on a phone booth which stood mere steps ahead of me ready for testing my hypothesis – spontaneously, I called my own number. The mobile phone rang. I pushed the call away – and as intended the voice mailbox jumped into motion and on the payphone I could hear: The announcement was indeed a personally recorded one, so callers were reacting to that – it wasn't by the Belgian whom I had bought the phone from, but by a woman speaking high-pitched and fast in an Asian language unknown to me. So much for my belief about cultural quirks and a special polite way unique to Australians for leaving voice messages – all that the callers really had intended was that their messages would really make it through to me.

Alternative payment methods accepted in the Northern Territory

Plastic boxes are an accepted currency! This I found out in the Northern Territory – for the first time at the Darwin Zoo. A friend of mine and me had banded together in order to travel to Perth together in his car. But there was an impediment which we had to tackle: Even without my luggage, both the car's trunk compartment as well as the space above the folded down back bench was cram-full, because (since he was a trained chef) he had gotten himself a fully equipped camping kitchen with everything one could require for cooking while travelling. To reduce weight and save fuel, before leaving the town for the Outback we cleared the car at our very first stop (the Darwin zoo parking place) of any contents he could spare: 15 empty food containers. We were at a loss as to what to do to get rid of them. Put them in a trash bin perhaps? But how – on a parking place without a single bin in sight? Besides that we deemed them to be too good for that. So we decided to gift them to the very first person we would encounter next. We met that person soon: It was the woman that operated the zoo's reception and pay desk (we wanted to visit it as first stop on our journey before venturing out into the wilderness). When purchasing tickets for us, we offered her the boxes. Spontaneously joking (as I sometimes do), I asked whether she would like to trade tickets for boxes. She threw them a scanning glance, looking them up and down once, then returned her eyes to the cash register, murmuring to herself for a few moments while pushing one button after another on it. This continued for some more moments and then all of a sudden, she finally looked up at us and happily announced our entry fee: In exchange for the containers, we got in for combined senior, student, family and school class discounts; all in all about 95% less than the full admission price for individual adults. Thus we got to pay with only very few small coins, yet still we were handed change!

Following that, while travelling through the Northern Territory, I asked each and every sales person that we encountered whether they would trade their goods for plastic containers, always explaining my question by narrating my experience at Darwin Zoo. Each of them laughed hearty amusement and enjoyed the story so much that they gave us gear and services in return without requesting any money at all – among that being fruit and vegetables, boastful souvenir bumper stickers from tiny settlements, medical treatment and a small Australian Aboriginal Flag which we attached to the hood of our car like a standard – many people past which we drove with it marveled at it with amazement or pride.

When I later travelled Southern Australia, such encounters with sales personnel went totally different: Upon hearing the story they always rolled their eyes, exclaimed with grave and slightly shocked faces "They're a bit different in the North" – and then immediately, without further thought about the story, charged me full price.

And again it was different in Victoria at the Melbourne Museum. Upon having told the story to the cashier (a senior, gray-haired citizen), he looked me over inquisitively with narrow eyes, then relaxed in an instant and promptly stated that I qualified for student discount, because without a doubt I must be one. Jovially and friendly he explained to me that proof for that to him were my hands, because they looked so delicate as if they never had done hard labor – to him these were a student's hands (I were so startled that I didn't mention that I had been doing hard work, albeit as an office clerk). So I got in for free. In a wide gesture, the cashier waved me onwards towards the railing. I kept my mouth shut and kept my amazement to myself as to why students weren't given a rebate as common elsewhere but entirely free entry. Instead I went with the wave and just ambled through the railing. I felt so happy, blessed and thrilled with gladness that I didn't take any special note of the fact that the railing had been standing wide open. Only much later did I learn that on that very day it was Melbourne museum's monthly day of open doors. Entry had generally been free on that day anyway, with all people being treated equally!

Plain car rental in the outback

I had reserved a rental car of the smallest category available from a station situated in a small outback town. Upon showing up at their office to pick it up, the rental agent surprised me by giving me a free upgrade to a much larger category – the reason being that this station was only holding cars of one single category available. Immediately I asked for additional insurance cover, being concerned that in case of any damage to a car which was much more sizable and expensive to replace than what I had selected, repair costs which I would have to bear would be much higher. But I were simply told by the rental agent not to bother – so he mentioned, absentmindedly, while printing out some forms. Next, he grabbed the forms, a clipboard and a pen, stepped out from behind his counter and asked me to follow him. I made a step backwards and two step sideways and there we were next to the car I was about to be given – so tiny were rental agency and adjacent car park. What followed next was the hand-over. We completed the paperwork standing right besides the car I were about to be given.

The rental agent skipped all of the forms on which existing damages had to be recorded. He didn't even glance at the forms or at the car which obviously had a couple of dents. Among those forms was one to be filled out upon return for recording (and subsequent invoicing) of any new damages inflicted to the car while it had been under my supervision. Yet a couple of days later when I were running late for the return date and called to ask for a postponement (especially since on top of the delay I still had to wash the car and refill the almost empty tank as required by what it said in the forms) the agent instead instructed me to just meet him in the town center the soonest I could make it there. When I arrived, he was sitting by the kerb waiting for me. He let me hand him the car keys and drove off to deliver it to the next customer.

Mom and the parkies

Those people we encountered in Darwin one late evening long after dusk really scared my mom. We were on our way from our hotel to a road lined with restaurants. In the tiny city center, all streets lay deserted. Only we were there – and those people; they just hung out on the sidewalk of a back road which was pretty much the sole route we could take. My mom spotted them and got tense immediately. Then she switched to walk on the other side of me so that I were between her and them, pulled her head between her shoulders and fixed her gaze upon the ground, even braced herself as if donning herself protection. Those people were startled. Stopped talking and gawk at her as we passed. They were native Australian descendants. Tall, wide and muscular – even gargantuan when compared to my mom's tiny slim figure. They seemed to be intoxicated and used to being so. The reason why they were standing and talking there? I couldn't recognize any. That first bad impression was reinforced later when we later saw them again: Now they were sitting on the lawn of a little park. As I were previously told by several Australians (who obviously had descended from European immigrants), these "parkies" still hadn't coped with the breakdown of their society and culture subsequent to colonization and thus were indulging in hanging around outdoors and getting intoxicated and that made them antisocial and potentially dangerous – so they told me and so I believed the warnings back then without double-checking. And quite clearly I weren't alone with that (albeit superficial) impression gained solely from the looks of those two situations, considering how frightened my mom seemed to be and how some light-skinned Australians (whom I've later came to regard as holding racist views) had told me their attitudes about aboriginal Australians without being asked. My second bad impression was even worse due to the fact that the little park we saw the parkies sitting in was doused in brightest floodlight even though it lay in a remote part of town which was void of people in the dead of the night – as if there had been intentions to put the parkies on stage to keep them from conducting mischief. But I contrast to that were the innocent, childlike looks on their faces and how quietly they were sitting there. (It wasn't until later that I came to know that it's common among Aboriginies – traditional even – to sit together outdoors.) Shortly after that encounter my mother and me visited a snack bar – at which I accidentally forgot my backpack. It wasn't until our return to our hotel that I got aware of the loss. I immediately returned to the snack bar, but by the time I got there it was gone. I turned to the people who were working there. They told me that they had seen it but not taken it into custody for me, believing that it's owner would take care of it himself. Someone else had taken it

Make a conscious effort to make it back home alive and healthy!

away and they hadn't bothered about that. Desperate, I ranged through the streets in search of it, returning to the hotel only briefly to fetch paper, pen and sticky tape in order to write and post missing announcements. There I informed my mother about what had happened and I agreed that she'd better stay in the hotel so she wouldn't get lost, yet later – after I had been running through the streets seeking for I can't say how much time – I did encounter her out there. She had opted to rather help me try to find it. We briefly spoke, then split up again and set off in different directions. After I don't how much further time of unsuccessful searching I finally gave in to the realization that I required help from professional searchers. Thus, I headed to the nearest police station. There, an officer helped me file a complaint and finally, the moment I signed the last document, the weight of it all fell off my shoulders, the stress vanished and a void filled my head – a void into which a thought, a worry spoke, first quietly but directly repeated with booming loudness: Where is my mom at this moment? I realized: My mom is somewhere out there! Alone in the dark! In an almost deserted town with only gargantuan, dangerously looking parkies around! Spontaneously, that realization took over my tongue and I burst out to the officer: "Now I just need to find my mom!" – Hearing that the officer looked up – face calm – looked past me, extended an arm to point at something behind me, saying: "Is that her there?" – I turned round. There, outsides the glass door, was my mom, peeking in. She was smiling gleefully and was surrounded by happy looking parkies. I joined them outsides. My mom's new pals had found her and taken her to the police station. They were more than glad to have been able to help her rejoin me and to guide and take care of her. This experience totally altered my views onto prejudices and foreigners. And until today I wonder: How did they manage to communicate with each other? Because my mother didn't speak English and the parkies didn't speak German. Obviously, well-meaning people understand each other without any words.

New Year's Eve – Frustration Not Fireworks

Would you like to see a huge multitude of very disappointed and homesick people from Germany? It's an easy feat: Venture out to any place located close to a city which gives panoramic views onto it. It's got to be shortly before midnight on New Year's Eve. That's what I did while I was in Perth, expecting to get to enjoy a display of fireworks similar to the ones I know from back home in Germany, where each year every person in every residential street celebrates by shooting up plenty of fireworks, amounting each year to a total of tens of thousands of tons. I weren't alone there at that vantage point in Kings Park, but became part of a horde of people who already stood there waiting. Some of them had made themselves comfortable, sitting in camping chairs whose type are typical to Australia. That gave me the impression to be among locals; seemingly this both validated my assumption and confirmed my expectation that I had come to the right spot for witnessing and enjoying a great show. With high hopes I stood among the crowd of people waiting in tense silence. Midnight – the turn of the year – was rolling closer fast now. When only fifteen further minutes of the old year were left, a small display of fireworks started at town hall square which was located far-away and below us. Viewed from the hill, it looked as small as a single freckle on a giant's face. It took place so far away you couldn't even hear it. Compared to what I had seen back home it was very minuscule. I mostly ignored it, smiling with anticipation for the large display of fireworks which certainly would come on soon and then go about outshining many times

Make a conscious effort to make it back home alive and healthy!

that candle-sized fireworks glinting in town hall square. In my mind, I fantasized about how the city landscape lying below us (currently only lit here and there in dim orange light by street lamps) would loudly be illuminated in sparkling colors dancing through the sky. I took a few pictures of the tiny fireworks display, but solely for practice. I deleted them immediately expecting that the real fireworks would start soon. Midnight came racing closer now and – passed. Without anything happening. The tiny fireworks display remained to be the sole one that night! When I finally realized that no other fireworks were likely to start, I hastily took more pictures of it – but this time with maximum zoom (which made it full frame, but – as I found later when reviewing them – blurred entirely). Still, the fireworks looked more like a single candle than (like fireworks in Germany do) a sky full of stars dancing all over it. Eventually the tiny display stopped – as silent and as unceremonious as it had started. Feeling severely disappointed, I set off immediately to walk back home. All the other attendants set into motion as well – only the people which were comfortably aseat in their camping chairs remained stationary, keeping to taking in the nightly cityscape panorama. Remembering how I had assumed them to be there for gazing at the fireworks – which was clearly over by now – that behavior puzzled me, so I stopped in my tracks, walked the few steps over to them and casually struck up a conversation, asking them how they had enjoyed the fireworks. While I spoke, I: Different from me they didn't seem to feet disappointed at all. Quite to the opposite – their reply was a simple: Fireworks? Turned out that they didn't seem to understand what I was actually talking about. They explained to me that they had come there solely to enjoy the view. Fireworks – yes, they couldn't have helped but notice that, but: not interested. It seemed to me as if they couldn't care less about that, which disproved my assumptions about this place being a good vantage point or that locals were interested in and put on fireworks. I then I turned away from the people who kept to enjoying the scenic view and took a few steps back to the road on which the crowd of people was heading back to town. That moment, when I saw the walking crowd, I really grasped just how little interested Australians are in celebrating with fireworks, because in the mass of walking people I discovered (besides mostly disappointed faces) that many of them were wearing brand name clothing which I knew from back home in Germany. I joined the crowd and addressed a few of people at random – in German. They replied in their and my native language and instantly told me how disappointed and disenchanted they were feeling. It downright blurted out of them how homesick they were feeling that moment and how badly they had been hoping to get to see a massive display of fireworks like the ones that you only get to see in Germany.

A turn off in The Outback

All of a sudden there was a traffic jam. Before that, we had been on the road alone for hours, driving through unsettled areas void of people – left and right of us only landscape which consisted solely (up until the faraway horizon) of gray-green shrub on yellow sand, above us a blue sky with large, light-gray clouds that hid the sun. We stopped the car, got out and walked towards the front of the traffic jam (about twenty meters further) and joined the people who were standing there staring into space next to their cars that stood motionless with all engines turned off. While walking, the surrounding air felt chilly on my bare arms. The closer I got to the front, the more of a truck with its blue tarpaulins became visible. It was lying on its side and across the entire road about thirty meters ahead of the line of vehicles. Standing around that truck were police cars, uniformed police officers – and that short queue of cars with people waiting next to them; a waiting line which had just grown by another vehicle thanks to my travel mate and me. At the front of said queue, I asked for an explanation of the surprising scene we had stumbled into and one of those waiting explained to me that the truck lying there had crashed long ago during the night before (now it was going onto noon) and that a crane truck was being waited for which was on its way there from the nearest town, Katherine, a couple hundred kilometers away. The crane truck was expected to arrive within a few more hours. Not keen on simply standing around doing nothing like the people there were, I made to walk back to our car. The sky meanwhile had clouded over so that everything around lay in a dusky light which cast no shadows. A coldish wind had come on. On that return walk I looked at the scenery around me and noticed that cars came down the road continuously, but nonetheless the queue wasn't growing! Those cars were turning off the road in a right angle onto the ground next to it, drove for about a dozen meters across that sandy plain, then took another turn at a right angle to drive across the plain in parallel to the road – until eventually they disappeared out of sight behind the crashed truck. Quite a lot of cars were in motion there – and coming from the other direction, too! There were so many that if it had been like that since the crash and if they all had queued, the traffic jam by now could have been several kilometers long, not twenty meters (plus our car) as it actually was. I found it astonishing how dense that off-road traffic was even though off the tarmaced road the ground consisted of only sand, bushes and nothing else: Cars were careering there bumper to bumper. It looked as busy as a trail of ants. Was that a way to dodge the traffic jam? But if so, why were there these drivers waiting which had formed a queue? I turned back to them and drew their attention to the cars turning off the road. Naturally they knew about it already (as they had been standing there for long enough, only meters away). They then told me how some off-road enthusiasts who had been in the queue had gotten impatient and set to check their maps on which they had discovered that located in the sand next to the road were older ones which had been abandoned when the new one had been built (the Australian way of building roads: forget about the past – it's a new day), with the outcome being what I had just spotted. But if so, I asked, then why was there a queue (albeit a rather brief one by the way when comparing it with the amount of traffic which continuously rushed past us off the road) if there was a way to circumnavigate the crash site? Their explanation was quite simple: The people in the queue didn't wanted to take their cars off the road. My travel mate and me however decided that we would follow the other cars. I walked ahead on feet to check if the ground was solid and flat enough for our heavily laden (and thus low lying) car while he would wait for my return and report. After just a few steps off the asphalt-black road and across the sand, I came across a second road with bleached gray surface. Past it – another few steps onwards – lay another road with intact yellow lines. It was on this road that plenty of cars drove past the crash site; it was almost as busy as in the Sydney city center on a Saturday night. I walked on it past the crash site; the drivers of the cars moving there only drove at walking speed and kept sufficient distance for me to feel safe. Seen from that spot in the plain, the queue and the crashed truck suddenly looked rather like a decorative still life – not anymore like a massive, insurmountable obstacle. The abandoned road was almost completely intact, only here and there could I spot a tiny pot hole, a crumbling edge or an overgrown sand heap. Finally, I reached the point beyond the crash site where the cars were turning off again to return to the new road. I turned around to head back and report to my travel mate, but almost stumbled into our car with him at the wheel. I walked to to the front door and he lowered the window and explained to me that he had seen a similarly laden, low lying car like ours, had deducted that he needn't wait for results of my observation and had set out to follow me. I climbed back into the car, we drove from the abandoned onto the regular road and then we were free again to venture on as much as we pleased, on a road now again almost void of cars and people, surrounded by wide open space.

Flying the flag

Australians are independent at heart. In the year 1977 by public plebiscite a new official national anthem was elected. The British "God save the Queen" was replaced by "Australia Advance Fair" (a rather formal sounding song). Runner-up in second place was "Waltzing Mathilda", a popular nursery rhyme which people favor since more than a hundred years ago as it tells a lot about Australian's attitudes and history. Australians like to chant it at official events right after the national anthem has been played. "Waltzing Mathilda" romanticizes a tale about a swagman worker who choses death over surrendering his freedom to authorities. The song has become widely known during a time when Australians as a society emancipated and developed a sense of civil and workers' rights. Uprisings were not unusual back then. The largest, most well-known uprising of all – and the sole one coming close to a revolution – took place in Ballarat, however it was overturned after just a few days. While the insurgents and their followers later effected some political changes, on location in Ballarat nothing much remained, or so it seemed to me at first. The restored, yet considerably damaged and aged flag of the insurgents (blue with a stylized southern cross) is conserved in the local museum behind glass in a dimly lit room. And the site where the insurgents had gathered, camped and held out is now covered with a fast food chain restaurant! How insensitive to history – or so I thought, until I noticed something in front of that branch which none of the other restaurants of that fast food chain have: a large, well-maintained lawn with a huge pole in its center. It's the largest flag pole near and far and from it flies a huge flag: the flag of the insurgents, a white southern cross on blue – true blue (which by the way is how Australian patriots describe themselves).

On a visit to the Melbourne Olympic Games museum

While I were on my way to the Melbourne Olympic games museum, I got to walk along a large and high-rising building site. It was a sports stadium into which one could look through a large opening as parts of the ranks had been torn down. While walking I was closely following the directions I had been given at Melbourne's tourist information center, but the further I got past the building site the more I worried that I might have missed the museum because according to the directions, I already should have arrived there. With growing confusion, I thought it'd be best if I'd turn to someone with knowledge of the area and inquire again for the whereabouts of the museum. Moments later, a group of men dressed in suits began to walk behind me. A few of them had taken off jackets and ties and each one of had donned a white and spotlessly clean builders hat. I figured they must somehow be part of the building site next to us and if so, chances were that they knew not just that site but a bit of the surrounding area as well, so I turned around spontaneously towards them and asked them if they could give me directions to the Olympic games museum. Immediately, one of them said "I'm, sorry!" He gestured towards the opening between the ranks, and explained: "We tore it down last week. But I'm personally inviting you to the reopening!"

On a visit to the Ballarat Olympic Games commemorative site

While I were on my way to the Ballarat Olympic Games commemorative site, two workmates gave me a ride in their car from the outskirts of Ballarat into the city center. It was during lunch break and they were heading for a restaurant. When I announced that I wanted to get dropped off way before that, they looked at me surprised and perplexed. But I was keenly pursuing another goal – I gladly shared my plans with them: to go and see the Olympic Games commemorative site. This information surprised them even more than what I had said before, since (as they told me) they were familiar with the Olympic Games which had been staged in neighboring Melbourne – but what on earth could have taken place in Ballarat, a small rural town more than a hundred kilometers far from Melbourne, the next large city? Those two had never before heard anything to that end at all. They spontaneously decided to alter their plans and join me. They even took took the trouble to drive a detour down side roads to see the monument for themselves. We found it standing by the shore of the lake where during the 1956 Olympic Games the rowing competitions had been staged. The monument looked quite frugal: a slender, about two and a half meters high stele, topped by the five rings, a fire bowl standing in front of it on a second, waist-high stele, all fashioned from white, crumbling plaster on steel-reinforced concrete. Just what one could realistically expect from a celebration of sports from a time before grand sponsors commercialized it. My two local companions however were (different from me) deeply impressed and both uttered intentions to return to this memorial to local history and bring their friends so they could enjoy the marvel, too.

Treats at the Coober Pedy train station

This story was told to me by the driver of a city tour who doubles as hotel shuttle jeep chauffeur. He showed us the sights of the area – the "salt and pepper hills" where "Pitch Black" had been filmed (a movie set in a colorful desert), the caves where Mad Max had been filmed (a movie set in a colorful desert), the local golf course with its signs which advise visitors to keep off the lawn (quite easily accomplished since the place consists only of – you guessed it – colorful desert) and plenty of mining rubble from the digging going on just about everywhere. He told us that many local people were searching for gemstones – even without official permits and including directly under their own houses! Because of that, many uncharted mine shafts exist in the region and thus the new railway line and station had been built distant from the town – right in the desert, about 40 kilometers distant from Coober Pedy. Eventually, at some point during that extensive city tour, the driver started to look as if he was daydreaming with open eyes and he told us a memory of his: a few nights ago he had went and picked up hotel patrons at Coober Pedy station, driving in the very same 4WD which we were sitting in at that moment. By the time he had successfully managed to drive all the way on the corrugated access road, the train had already long been gone – so long ago that it had not just moved onwards but even disappeared beyond the horizon (which lay in clear view since only shrubs grow in that desert). The train station consists only of a platform adjacent to the single line railway track. It was there where his three passengers (and only them) were waiting for him. And to his pleasant surprise, they had brought him something! They had done so because while the train had been approaching their target destination, they had been sitting in the restaurant car, had been feeling very snug and pampered (partially out of joyful anticipation of the favor and luxury of the hotel shuttle service by said driver) and had spontaneously decided to show him their appreciation and gratitude. Therefor, just before getting off they told their story to waitstaff and asked if there was something they could bring along as a treat for the shuttle driver. There was, and so they had asked for it to be added to their bill and carefully carried it while deboarding with all their luggage. And so he encountered his three passengers: Standing at night alone with themselves and their luggage under a clear, star strewn black sky, in the middle of a sandy desert lit by the bright light of a full moon, on an otherwise empty platform lying next to an empty single-line railway track that extended straight across the nightly desert from one horizon to the opposite one – they were holding out to him: a glass of freshly poured, still sparkling champagne.

ACKNOWLEDGMENTS

Thanks to...

...Mandy. Without her travel appetite and encouragement, this book would still be in my head.
...my parents for sponsoring me onto the journey.
...Kathy of Apple Island Naturals (www.appleisland.ca) for reviewing the first edition.
...the people who made, operate or produce content for dict.leo.org, dict.cc, Google Translate, linguee.de, langenscheidt.de, thesaurus.com, merriam-webster.com, oxforddictionaries.com – and the Google image search (which is always a good way to confirm that the words I use for descriptions do convey the images which I want to get across).
...Queensland Department of National Parks, Tasmania Parks and Wildlife Service, New South Wales National Parks & Wildlife Service, Cancer Council Australia, Transport Accident Commission, National Roads & Motorists' Association, Transport for New South Wales – Road Safety Center, Queensland Government – Department of Environment and Heritage Protection, Northern Territory Emergency Service and Surf Life Saving Australia – for sharing their advices with me.
...all the fabulous people I've met during my travels – especially those who helped me stay safe and sound, such as restaurant attendants handing out to me liter upon liter of water, cave guides getting me back to the light of day, road construction workers who've built guardrails and have painted "look right" onto road crossings, police officers, tour guides, bus drivers, hostel crew members, sunscreen vendors, park guides who took their time to explain repeatedly local dangers in meticulous detail, reliable vehicle maintainers, good travel mates, that elderly lady which was my seat

neighbor on an Moree-bound train who encouraged me to "call mom", flight attendants doing the security advice ballet before every lift off – and to all the poisonous animals for leaving me alone.

...and, finally, to the expat who, upon hearing about my intentions to visit her home country, strongly recommended that I pack a jumper.

ABOUT THE AUTHOR

Rainer Krauhs is a cautious office worker, spending his day programming computers. At one time in his life he has dared to venture out into the wilderness. Only in retrospect did he realize how naivety had put him into mortal danger – this book is the outcome of that. Rainer Krauhs is back at the desk, living and writing in Hamburg, Germany. He has just finished studying for an MBA with the Open University Business School and can't hardly wait to venture out into the world again. Could you help him pay for flight tickets? Please recommend this book.